escape

The definitive guide to
escaping the rat race,
starting a business
and becoming a
FreedomPreneur™

Amanda C. Watts

RETHINK PRESS

First published in Great Britain 2016
by Rethink Press (www.rethinkpress.com)

Praise

"Escape! The Definitive Guide To Escaping The Rat Race, Starting A Business And Becoming A FreedomPreneur is what EVERY person with raging fire in their soul needs to read to create the life and the long-awaited freedom they deserve. No bullshit. It teaches you HOW, thankfully, because all you've considered so far is WHY. These are real life lessons, not just theories. If you want to escape, you have no excuse to be ignorant about the tenacious journey taken by those who have been there and can teach you how to do it. Learn well. Get in the fast lane. Pursue your dreams fearlessly and use the *Escape* book as your best friend, your guide; it's going to be the best partner in crime you ever had."

Michael Serwa

www.michaelserwa.com

"This is not a book but a manual. A manual that takes you from what you are today, struggling, stressed and massively dissatisfied, and rebuilds you into the ultimate FreedomPreneur! Step by step it will replace all your tired old parts and rebuild you into a premium-operating machine so you will never have to look back at your old life. Your life as a FreedomPreneur is closer than you think – grasp it now!"

Jagdeep Lota

www.jagdeeplota.com

"You need to read this book! If you're thinking of starting a business or already in a business and feel overwhelmed or just want to take your business to the next level, then this is the book for you! I loved reading this book but now cannot wait to start reading it again; it's going to be a great reference book throughout my life to help keep me checking my goals and passions so that my business is still aligned with these. Amanda's book is a road map for you to begin to live your life of freedom!"

Kathy Bees, ACMA, CGMA

www.rsgk.co.uk

"The reality of business success is that plenty of people have done it before us – the rest of us just need to work out how to copy it. In her book, Amanda provides this plan and tells her personal story as the perfect motivation and inspiration for you to leave the rat race. Around it is woven practical activities from notable experts and Amanda's own experiences that you can follow as your path to success. I always need refreshing and this book did it in an accessible and powerful way."

Jonnie Jensen

www.liveandsocial.com

"This book is a blue-print for success. Amanda C. Watts gives you everything you need to take your business idea and turn it into reality. Straightforward and to the point, she shows you not only what you need to do and how to do it but also how you need to think to realise your dreams. This is more than just a 'how to' book though as there are workbooks and sheets to guide you through the process and help put those ideas into practice. It's motivational and uplifting tone inspires you to take the leap and become the FreedomPreneur you know you can be."

Nicola Laurie

www.mstidyowl.co.uk

"Amanda C. Watts is uniquely qualified to help you escape your day job to becoming a FreedomPreneur. I have sat back and watched her trail blaze her work now for almost two years and also collaborated with her be part of the #1 personal development book series in the world, *The Change*. Amanda knows how to transform people and get results. Her new book, *Escape*, will be another huge success! If you are really wanting to break through your limitations that are holding you back, read this book and share it with others who are sharing the same space as you and are ready to launch their own business. Amanda has created a new space for men and women alike to become who they really are meant to be. She's spearheading a new path for many to follow!"

Deborah Crowe

www.debcrowe.com

"WOW! This is a great book! So easy to read. Amanda talks to you in a way that is on-the-level and inspirational at the same time. I couldn't put it down! It is full of handy hints and tips to help you focus on your niche: your WHY.

The exercises help to get you thinking and it is full of examples, both personal and of other people's journeys. It has lots of inspiring quotes to get you thinking too. This book had my pulse racing, urging me to get on and get going NOW!

It really is a MUST HAVE for anyone, no matter who you are or what you do. If you want to start your business and live your life of freedom, it all starts here!"

Pascale Lane

www.TeenMindsetLondon.co.uk

"I took the plunge and started my business because of Amanda C. Watts. I met her back in 2013 when I was employed. We clicked, she shared and I grew just by knowing her. I started my business while I was still employed and Amanda was my first client. She taught me about social media, which as it turned out I had a flare for just like she did, but more than that she encouraged me to 'do it'. Amanda shared her tools, her knowledge and templates to help me build a virtual assistant business. Much of what she shares in *Escape* she kindly and generously gave to me and nine months after meeting her, LBB Business Solutions was a reality full time."

Lindsey Brown Burden

www.brownburden.com

"This book is the 'kick up the bum' that will get you out of the rat-race into the life you'll love. Every word resonates with Amanda's energy and enthusiasm. She's been there, and done it. Follow her advice, and you can do it too. Do it, do it, do it."

Jackie Barrie

www.jackiebarrie.com

"This book is priceless. It's structured in such a way that makes the mountain of information you need to learn and apply, easier to process. There are a million things to think about when starting and building your business, and in this book you will find exercises, systems and tasks that will answer all your questions about how to do it and make it work. This book is not just a book, it's like a university marketing manual, but it's for the real world, to implement rather than just learn the theory. It's a manual you will go back to again and again."

Alexandra Merisoiu

www.themerisoiutechnique.com

"This book is jam packed full of useful insights, quality tips and step-by-step guides for the aspiring business owner. This book is an effective blueprint to starting to build a business you truly love!"

Chris Daems

www.cervellofp.co.uk

"Are you're sitting in an office with the idea of becoming your own boss, running a successful company and generally dreaming of making the seemingly impossible leap from cubicle monkey to master of your own destiny? Well you are in luck because Amanda has created an essential piece of the puzzle by writing her book *Escape*. Throughout the book she shares the many steps in her struggle to start her own business and the lessons she learned first-hand. In business if you want to know something you either have to learn the hard way or have someone looking out for you who can prevent you making the big mistakes. Get this book, keep it close to hand, read it cover-to -over and use it whenever you get stuck. Amanda has written an invaluable guide for all those currently stuck in employment hell with a dream of a better life. I say, get this book and go for it!"

Stu Morrison

www.mistermetric.com

Amanda C. Watts has successfully crystallised all the elements of what it means to be a success as a FreedomPreneur in business for yourself right now. A combination of clearly defined strategy together with the brutal honesty of real life experience makes for a truly inspirational read. Packing an extra punch of high value practical accountability in the form of interactive worksheets, Amanda quite literally crafts your lifestyle business with you from the very first word."

Paul.D.Atherton

UK Sales Coach of the year www.StressLessSales.com

What is a FreedomPreneur™?

We have coined the phrase FreedomPreneur™ here in the UK.

A FreedomPreneur™ is a passionate and hungry entrepreneur who runs a business on their terms.

A FreedomPreneur™ is a life enthusiast who creates a business to give themselves freedom, to do what they love and blaze their own path to follow their dreams – whatever that means to them.

A FreedomPreneur™ can be a workaholic (because that's what they love) or have a 4-hour workweek. For us it means having a business that enables us to spend a lot of time with our two children. For others it means a laptop lifestyle, working from exotic places and soaking up the sun as they work.

A FreedomPreneur™ writes their own rules, they have escaped the rat race, started a business and made following their passions their full time job.

Contents

Dedication

This book is dedicated to all those who have supported me throughout my life and on my mission to freedom.

My mentors and coaches who have patiently watched and guided me on this amazing journey.

My clients who have become my friends, implemented what I teach in this book and created their own freedom-based lives.

My parents who let me follow my passions and do what I love, even if it meant skipping college lessons to sunbathe and hang out on Brighton beach.

My sister Fiona and brother-in-law Mark who have kept me grounded and supported me through the hard and fun times.

My best friend Pascale who has been my rock for over twenty years.

My husband Matthew who has watched me transition from entrepreneur to FreedomPreneur and loved and supported me through my failures and wins.

And last but not least, my dear children Joshua and Annabelle. You are my everything and my reason for being. If I can teach you one thing in life it is to live with passion and freedom.

Introduction

If you think it's about starting a business you are missing the point. It's about creating a life of freedom.

The world has changed. Opportunities are now everywhere, and everybody and anybody can change their life, if they are determined enough.

However, according to Deloitte's Shift Index Survey, 80% of people are dissatisfied with their jobs. But so few of these people actually make the leap and do something that they are passionate about.

A select few find the gumption and courage to change their life. They make it their mission to live a life filled with more freedom to do what they want, with whom they want, and live where they want. They live a life on their terms.

We call these people FreedomPreneurs.

A FreedomPreneur is different to an entrepreneur. When I escaped my corporate job it was because I was burnt out, unhappy and stressed. I was bordering on depression and I found my life was spent keeping up with the Joneses.

I had spent years climbing the corporate ladder. I was first in, last out. I worked sixteen-hour plus days to build somebody else's dream and vision. I had sold *my* dreams for a six-figure paycheque. I was no more than a slave.

In 2009 I launched my own business and called myself an entrepreneur. My business became the focus of my life. Day in, day out, I would get up early and go to bed late. I worked seven days a week and long hours. The business was my priority and I was tired, unhappy and stressed. Building the business was hard work; I became a slave to it. It was no different from my corporate job, except I didn't have the steady paycheque.

In 2012 I decided that enough was enough. I had two children aged seven and nine and I wasn't seeing them as much as I should. I figured that there must be a better way to live.

I decided that instead of struggling and stressing, it was time to hustle and juggle – hustle hard at set times, and juggle the business with my life the rest of the time. It was time to take back control and live a life of freedom. It was no longer acceptable to be trapped as an entrepreneur; I made it my mission to become a FreedomPreneur, living a life filled with passion, doing what I loved, and embracing what the word freedom meant to me.

Being a FreedomPreneur gives you the ability to decide what you want out of life and make following your passions your full time job. Being a FreedomPreneur means you can take your children to and from school every day.

Being a FreedomPreneur means that you get to have month long holidays in the summer. It means your business shuts down for at least two weeks over Christmas if you desire.

Being a FreedomPreneur means that you can work from anywhere in the world.

We have been playing small

We have been conditioned from a young age to do well at school, get good grades, go to college, go to university, get a good job at a great firm and have powerful careers.

It is this conditioning that keeps us playing small. We are led to believe that we are doing well in life when in actual fact we feel that something is missing. We are successful on the outside, but numb on the inside. We live our lives in hues of grey, when in fact a life of freedom can be glorious Technicolor.

Right now the idea of making the leap and setting up your own business may seem daunting. But I want to assure you that your years of experience and knowledge, and your life in the corporate world, will serve you well when you make the leap. You can earn six or even seven figures by packaging up your talents and expertise and doing what you love.

At this moment in time it may seem farfetched. Maybe you have run your business ideas past family and friends and they have shot you down. If this is the case I want you to ignore the naysayers and really tap into what you love, and your passions. It's time for you to get a little self-belief.

You may well have seen the people who have already made the leap from employee to freedom. These people are the ones you see speaking at events all over the world. They are shouting from the rooftops about what they believe in, working from far off shores and have time to do Yoga by the sea between working. They are the happy mums at the school gate who are in charge of their destiny, running their own businesses and taking time off to spend with their children most afternoons.

These people have escaped their corporate jobs and are helping the world become a better place while sipping on mocha lattes in Starbucks. These people are FreedomPreneurs.

They are no different from you; they have just taken the simple yet profound step to change their lives. They have packaged up their passions, talents, stories and experiences and are helping solve other people's problems.

FreedomPreneurs are business and life coaches, relationship consultants, marketing strategists, web designers, photographers, videographers, interior designers, accountants... the list is endless. And they all have one thing in common: they are passionate about what they do.

In 2012 I changed the way I worked and went from entrepreneur to FreedomPreneur. I pivoted my business, changed whom I helped and how I helped them, and designed my own life.

It became clear as I coached others to launch and grow businesses that there was a simple methodology behind a freedom-based business. This methodology has been used by thousands of people across the globe and enables them to do what they love, and it is this methodology that I share with you in this book today.

This book contains life-changing strategies

There are two kinds of business book readers in the world. The serial reader likes to read book after book, inhaling information yet never really understanding that if just one of the actions in the book were implemented, they could create a successful business.

The other kind of book reader is the action taker, who devours books with passion and implements with determination. I have added some extra resources if you are the devourer. Throughout this book you will find the opportunity to download worksheets and programmes that will enable you to get the most out of the information.

I have written this book in a particular order for a reason. Upon your first read, I recommend you read the chapters in the order they are written. Once you have completed the book, go back and start actioning each of the steps outlined. After that you can dip in and out of the chapters, using the information as you need it.

Everything I have included in this book got me to my amazing life today. It is what enables my family and me to live a life filled with passion, doing what we love. There is no mumbo jumbo; nothing that is so difficult to implement that you will want to give up. You will be able to read the book, complete the worksheets and make the leap from corporate employee to FreedomPreneur.

Your life filled with passion, purpose and prosperity starts here.

Do great things.

A FreedomPreneur's Mindset

Powerful You

No book can give you a set of instructions to guarantee your success. If I could guarantee success I would be charging millions for this information.

Your success will increase exponentially, however, if you embrace the principles and strategies outlined in this book.

Ready? Let's get on with part one of your escaping your day job and starting a business.

If you could choose to do anything, and knew you would be highly successful at it, what would you choose?

- Would you continue with what you have been doing? Or would you pivot and change direction?
- Would you hand your resignation in right now, if guaranteed no money worries and a life filled with passion?
- Would you launch your dream business?
- Would you escape the cubicle?
- Would you do what you are meant to do, live your purpose and make a difference?

I want you to imagine that you have just been guaranteed this success. Read this book believing that you will succeed and achieve all that you put your mind to. Embrace the proven techniques. Action what you learn. Change your life forever.

Throughout this book I will outline powerful ideas that will get you to success. Your success lies within you; it is you who will make or break your business idea. Not the economy, not the idea itself, and certainly not how many times you post on social media.

It's decision time. You are either in or out. I urge you to make the decision to succeed at whatever you choose to do in life. Never give up, no matter what.

The mindset of a successful person

Who do you need to become to be successful on your terms?

There are two mindsets: fixed and growth. Fixed mindset people assume that they know everything already. Growth mindset people understand that they can learn and tweak what they are doing.

By picking up this book to explore your options, you have already shown you have something of a growth mindset. We are going to explore working on your mindset further in this part of the book. I recommend you do not skip this part. Without understanding your mindset, you will find the life of a FreedomPreneur difficult. FreedomPreneurs think differently, act differently, and behave differently to employees. But the change is small. I am talking about a tweak of 2mm.

If more than half of all businesses fail within the first five years, how do you ensure that your business is not one of them?

It all starts with *you*.

The 2mm Rule – excellent to extraordinary

The 2mm I mentioned is the difference between excellent and extraordinary. Let me explain this using Tiger Woods as an example. Tiger Woods was excellent. But when he got himself a coach and tweaked his golf swing by 2mm he became extraordinary.

If you can tweak how you feel, act and look by 2mm, you too can go from excellent to extraordinary. Imagine if you lifted your shoulders and chest by 2mm. You would feel more empowered. You would look more confident.

Average, good, better, best, excellent and extraordinary all vary. At the beginning, you require a big leap to go from average to good. But towards the end, just a minor adjustment of 2mm will take you from excellent to extraordinary.

So what are our 2mm moments? These are the tiny things we can do to stand out from the rest and make our lives extraordinary. At work you may be a high performer and have probably plateaued at best to excellent. Your goal would have been to put your stamp on all you do, and do a good (or better, best, excellent) job. To live a life of freedom and start your own successful business, you will need to crank it up by a tiny 2mm.

In our everyday life, comfort can become our definition of bliss. We wake up in our house (a box) and drive our car (a box) or get on the train (a box) to work in our office (a box), then we eat lunch (out of a box), return to our office (a box), catch the train home (in a box to our box), all to relax by turning on the box! It's all a bit samey and boring, and keeps us from having an extraordinary life.

If you want to have a life of freedom and be an extraordinary FreedomPreneur, it's time to embrace the 2mm rule.

Extraordinary people do things differently. They earn money doing things they are passionate about, are in control of their destinies and make a difference to the world.

Extraordinary people don't watch too much TV to escape from their 'boxed' lives. They are not entertained by the programmes and don't fall prey to the advertisements – extraordinary people do not get influenced easily to buy things they don't need.

Extraordinary people are about play and purpose. They live a life of freedom and are far less likely to drink often, smoke or get addicted to drugs.

Extraordinary people track time. They don't just live in the moment; they think about the future rather than instant gratification.

Extraordinary people are not lazy. If they were, they would not have time to be extraordinary. They take action and don't suffer from procrastination.

Extraordinary people don't live for their lie-ins at the weekend. They jump out of bed and follow their passions and purpose, with purpose!

Extraordinary people don't wait for flashes of inspiration. They take action and create their destiny, acting on their dreams.

Extraordinary people don't assume anything. They explore options and take nothing as fact. They go the extra 2mm to master what they know and do totally.

Extraordinary people have a growth mindset. They don't give up when they fail in a task or even a business. They learn from their failures and get better and better. In fact, extraordinary people love to fail. If you are not growing, you are dying, and failure means growth.

Extraordinary people know that the hand they were dealt when they were born does not have to be what they are stuck with. They know they can go after an extraordinary life.

In my opinion the reason so many business ideas fail is because the majority never even make it out of a person's mind. Extraordinary people do extraordinary things because they turn their thoughts into reality. This is how they achieve success.

I have spent the last ten years studying successful and extraordinary people and entrepreneurs. I truly believe that there is an underlying theme to the lives these people live.

Why are some people more successful than others?

The simple answer is because successful people don't want to live the status quo. They need more, they give more, they learn more, they share more. They avoid average at all costs.

They do this through mastering their actions and managing their mindset. Change your mind, change your destiny.

What do great leaders like Tim Cook, Warren Buffet, Sir Richard Branson and Oprah Winfrey have in common? The answer is quite simple: they are powerful. From the inside out.

Some say performance and success are predetermined and limited to a few exceptional people. I say 'some' are wrong. Inside every truly successful person is a deeply ingrained purpose – a purpose that carries them forward, day after day. This purpose drives their performance.

Everyone has the ability to tap into their purpose and motivate themselves to get out of bed in the morning to do something bigger than the sum of one. Everyone has the ability to live their dreams on their terms. But you have to envisage, believe, set goals, plan and take action on your dreams.

Nothing was going to stop Sir Richard, Warren or Oprah. They had a big mission, and believed it could happen. And if they can do it, so can you.

Success happens to those who relentlessly strive for it. Success happens to those who get knocked down then quickly jump up again ready for round two, round three and round fifty. Success comes to those who never, ever give up.

Everyone is looking for an edge in today's unpredictable and competitive marketplace. While people perform well when things are going in their favour, many people don't perform well when under pressure. What is needed is the ability to perform more and more highly in any given situation. Tapping into the powerful you will certainly help with this.

In the following pages I will outline traits you may already have, and some that will possibly need work.

Believe In Yourself And Your Idea

Once you believe in something,
you will actually embody it.

Come with me on a journey. Imagine you were in a coma...

One day you wake up with no memory. You have no idea of what your life used to be like. Upon awakening, the nurses tell you that you were a Royal Marine, and a highly decorated one at that.

How do you think you would feel about yourself?

It may cross your mind that you were a great leader, a quick decision maker, full of integrity, courage and knowledge. You may feel pride that you were a Marine and immediately embody these traits.

On the flip side, imagine upon wakening you are told you were a road sweeper. What would your initial thoughts be?

What you believe you are is who you are.

One job title would make you swell with pride, immediately putting you in a state of confidence and feeling powerful. The other would feel less empowering. Your actions would then change depending on which career you embodied.

And this is why belief in yourself and your idea is imperative.

The belief system

If you don't believe in yourself and your ideas, then who will? If your belief system is shot to pieces, then your relationships, job, and overall life will seem unfulfilled.

It is all about having the proper belief system about who you are. Before others believe in you, you must believe in yourself. You must truly believe you are unique and special. Because there is no one quite like you.

> *'Today you are you, that is truer than true. There is no one alive who is youer than you.'*
> DR SEUSS

I need to drive this point home. Here is another example:

Imagine you are an actor. You are off to an audition. *You* truly believe inside yourself that you are one of the best actors in the world. Because you believe you are the best, your expressions, tone of voice, the way you speak are all highly convincing. The result is that people relate to you as you present yourself.

However, now imagine you've had hundreds of knock-backs. You have been turned away for the smallest of parts and are desperate for this acting job. Because of this, you are nervous; you speak without conviction and are resigned to the fact that you probably won't get the part.

Our brain is a circuit – our success all depends on how we are wired.

If we introduce the proper wiring, then our brain works brightly. If we are unsure about who we are and do not believe in ourselves then our dreams will never become a reality.

Overcoming negative thoughts

Back to Sir Richard, Warren and Oprah. Do you believe that they are positive all the time? No. It is not possible to be truly positive all the time. Not unless you live in La-la Land.

Even the most successful people have times when negative thoughts enter their mind, but they *never* dwell on these thoughts. The successful take actions to overcome any problems they may be having and consciously accentuate the positive.

I cannot stress enough how much action overcomes fears and problems. This was a hard lesson for me to learn as I was growing my business. There were weeks when I made no sales. There were weeks when I was so busy I didn't know what to do with myself and sat on my chair, overwhelmed. There were weeks when I just wanted to run and hide.

But I worked on my mindset. I found a way to overcome the negative thoughts.

Now if I have a problem, then I need to counteract that problem. And taking positive action immediately overcomes problems, at the same time making me feel much better too.

You and your belief system

We are all born with the ability to feel confident and happy. We are born believing we can do anything.

You only need to look at a small child and see the way it laughs confidently and loudly. Look at the way a child moves through the streets and green fields with ease; the way it climbs trees. Children are born without inhibitions. They sing and dance like there is nobody watching.

It is only as we grow that our surroundings, environment, parents, teachers, friends and acquaintances start to shape the people we are today.

As we go from infant to child or teenager to adult, we pick up what people say, learning habits, family traits and new belief systems.

It is the beliefs we learn which hold us back in later life. We create a map of the world that has been conditioned over our lifetime. This belief system determines whether we are happy, depressed, excited or bored.

It is purely our belief system that determines our courage, fears and behaviours. It affects everything that we do. It determines our current success, health, wellbeing and the quality of our relationships.

There is no getting away from it. Our belief system is always on autopilot. It is made up of facts that we take for granted. It determines whether we will be rich or poor, average or extraordinary.

A belief system could include:
- Eating healthily will bring me good health
- Smoking is bad for me
- I am going to be poor
- Money is the root of all evil
- I am going to be rich
- Women who wear too much makeup are shallow
- Gluten is bad for me
- As I get older it's easier to put on weight.

Can you see how these beliefs will affect your actions every day?

How you can change your belief system

I have great news. If your current belief system is not serving you well, you can change it – if you have the desire to change it.

Your belief system is more than your thoughts. It is more than just how you think about things. It is your deep-seated emotions: what you like, dislike, your opinions and fears. Even what you smell is driven by your belief system.

This is demonstrated countless times when people, under hypnosis, believe that an onion smells like an apple, and can be eaten as if it were an apple too.

If your belief system is not serving you well, what are the steps to changing it?

How do you change the number one thing that determines success or failure in your business venture?

These are powerful questions.

Unpleasant thoughts are usually due to two factors: fear of our personal safety and wellbeing, which can include our financial situation, and fear that we are not as good, moral, strong, rich or beautiful as our partner, friends, family and the wider community want us to be.

In other words, our unpleasant thoughts are usually stemmed in failure – either trying to avoid it or believing it will hurt us, or others.

Our priority is to have enough food and water to survive. After food and water, we need to feel safe and secure. This merges with the need to belong and have family and friends. Contrary to popular belief, we are not hardwired to be competitive; more we want to feel loved, valued and part of a relationship, family group or community.

I want you to remember this when you are creating your business. Just as we want to belong, so will our clients. Seth Godin refers to this as being part of a tribe. We either want to be part of it, or have a yearning to lead the tribe. Business owners often tend to be the leaders.

If you have unpleasant thoughts, you may be missing a piece of the jigsaw puzzle. You may be needing to feel more secure and safe; to have more of a feeling of belonging. Many want to leave their corporate job as they feel they don't belong. Many stay unfulfilled in their corporate job because they don't want to risk the secure feeling it gives them.

When you understand why you are feeling a certain way, you can work out how to feel more positive and less scared.

Tools for changing your thoughts and feelings

Your belief system is made up of what you have been telling yourself for years and years. It is learnt behaviour. So you can unlearn it, and reprogram it.

You can turn any unpleasant thoughts and negative feelings into positive affirmations. You can recite these affirmations over and over to yourself until they become ingrained in your belief system; your new normal.

You can change your mind, and therefore change your destiny.

Program Your Mind For Success

Success is no accident. Success happens when:

- You have a big why
- You set goals to achieve your why
- You believe you can achieve your why
- You take action to achieve your why.

Success doesn't happen when you sweat the small stuff and get stuck.

Many of my clients take years to pluck up the courage to launch their own business. Some come to me after a marriage breakdown, having missed too much family time, or having suffered ill health. The thing that stopped them coming to me sooner was fear, often of things like:

- How do I get a website?
- Where do I find my clients?
- How do I use social media – what the heck is Twitter?
- What happens if I fail?

If you have a big enough Why you can overcome the How. First step is to set goals. Big goals that are aligned with your passions, purpose and your big Why.

I cannot stress enough how much you will squash your dreams if you sweat the small stuff. It will stop you from changing your mindset. It will keep you dreaming, but not achieving. You can learn to outsource the small stuff.

Just like who you believe you are determines who you become, what you believe you can achieve will determine your achievements. Set a goal. Once you believe that the goal can be achieved, then the path will be revealed.

Success is no accident. Living an incredible life is no accident. To live an incredible life you have to do it on purpose. You can only live on purpose when you know exactly who you are, what it is you want to achieve, why you want to achieve it, and then take action to achieve it.

Let me repeat that:
- Know who you are
- Know what you want to do
- Know why you want to do it
- Take action.

Find the powerful you

Deep inside, you already have all the answers to realise your power. You are still you, even if you have given up much of you as the years rolled by and your thoughts became part of someone else's belief system.

It's now time to tap back into the authentic you. We are going to reignite the fire in your tummy to live a life that you love, a life of freedom, every day. It's time to escape the cubicle.

If you love what you do, and do what you love, day in, day out, you will never work a day in your life again.

Some people are at their most powerful when they are working for someone else, and they love every minute of doing so. They become a success in their own right while working for a company. They may not be the founder, but they feel part of the business.

They strive to make a success of each day, and they strive for their satisfaction and the good of the company. These people are powerful. These people are probably not reading this book as one doesn't tend to read what doesn't interest one.

But you are not 'one'. You are done with building someone else's dream. You have dreams of your own. You are seeking freedom.

I'm talking about creating a business that you love. Doing something that matters to you: work that fills your heart with joy and makes the world a better place.

It's time for you to leave a legacy.

Find your Why

On my personal development journey I stumbled across a man called Simon Sinek. He speaks of inspiring others and finding your big Why.

If you set yourself a big goal, you need to understand why this goal is important. Once you get clear on what you want to achieve, it is crucial for your success to know why you want to achieve it.

It is only your Why that will drive you.

The big Why is the start of you becoming powerful. It is the important catalyst for you to overcome any 'how', and will give you the determination for you to succeed.

Most people are too focused on the how and they miss the important why, which is why most people never succeed. You will not be most people.

When it comes to investing our precious time, money and

resources into something, we have to have a big reason for doing so. It makes a huge difference if our reason is strong. If we have enough reasons for the goal, we exponentially increase our chances of success. The Universe hangs on to the answers we seek until it is convinced that we are inspired enough by our desire to succeed. When our desire is equal to the task, we find what we are looking for.

Our why is often a mixture of our passions and the feeling of purpose inside us. Our why is our mission.

Find your passion

> *'Passion is energy. Feel the power that comes from you focusing on what excites you.'*
> OPRAH WINFREY

You are the only one who can find your passion. It is deep inside you, and just has to be uncovered and awakened.

Occasionally I find someone who knows why they were put on this earth and has a deep rooted sense of purpose and passion. Once I learnt about the importance of basing a business on my passions and purpose, business became easy. But more often than not people have to search for what they are passionate about. They have to ask a series of questions to help them uncover their truth.

My biggest passion in life is creating something from ideas that I have come up with, or helped others come up with. I love the feeling inside of me when I have life changing ideas and solutions. It is a powerful high to love what you do.

But I didn't always know that this is what sets me alight. Having worked in marketing since 1993, I found it hard to find exactly where I fitted in the business world. I tried working in exhibitions, the hospitality industry, health and wellness and with coaches. It was only when I actually looked at the gifts I have been given in this world and analysed what I loved that I had my eureka moment.

The Eureka! moment

Your eureka moment often becomes your business niche. (You may want to write that down for when you get further into the book.)

The day I had my eureka moment, an excitement started that built up inside me over the subsequent weeks and months until it was unstoppable. It was like everything fell into place: my life went from hard work to ease. By finding my passion I had uncovered a huge part of my why.

Having spent years working in a dull, unfulfilling nameless corporate environment, creating brochures, marketing campaigns and writing copy, I at last was fulfilled and happy.

I had struggled my whole corporate career to be recognised, seen, and to get the pay rises and promotions I'd worked hard for. I was the first in and last out. I worked sixty to seventy hour weeks building someone else's dream. At first the bosses had tried to fool us that it was a team effort, but as their business grew and they became more successful, the less happy I and the other employees were.

To the outside world I was successful. At the age of twenty-five I was earning a small fortune, travelling the world, driving around in a brand new convertible car, living in a modern flat minutes from the centre of London. But inside I was empty.

This feeling of emptiness led to a series of very poor decisions. When I had the opportunity to escape my corporate life and marry an army officer, give up my career and have babies, I jumped at it. I was burnt out and exhausted. Anything seemed better than having to work seventy hours a week for no recognition.

But a funny thing happened. It didn't make me happy. I had married 'well' (to outsiders), but still on the inside I was unhappy. The same pattern of behaviour manifested itself in my marriage, and I was again ready to jump ship and escape.

To help me feel more fulfilled I started helping small local businesses with marketing – for free. From my home in Somerset (I'd fled London) I created a marketing consultancy where I helped advise the mums and dads I'd met on my travels who had their own businesses. I may have tried to escape corporate, but I was still passionate about business.

After leaving my unhappy marriage I was too scared to set up a business, so I got a part time job. I had no money, didn't feel safe and secure and was lonely. I got married a second time when I was offered security and love, but again this marriage failed. I was making bad decision after bad decision.

The day I left my second marriage, with two children, a car and their belongings, was the day I changed. I remember sitting in my parents' bathroom crying my eyes out, not with sadness, but with anger. Anger that I had put myself and my children in situations that we shouldn't have been in. I was so busy being concerned with external factors in my life (possessions, people's opinions, etc.) that I was mucking everything up.

I remember the day well. I had never felt so bad. Yet I also felt a feeling of hope, and change. I knew I was going to start a life that had never been so extraordinary. I decided that I had to change; my life depended on my actions, not those of the people around me. I was the only one who could create an amazing life for me and the children.

I was technically homeless with no money, no clothes and no job. It was decision time.

I could either go back to the hard faceless corporate world of stress, burnout and guaranteed wage, or start my own business.

I was scared.

As I said before, it is our beliefs in life that will determine our success. And I was fortunate enough to believe I could do it on my own. So I made the leap and started my own business. I was an official corporate escapee, on my own terms.

And I set up a copywriting agency.

What?

Yes, at the time I thought that was what I needed to do. My belief system told me that I didn't know enough about marketing and business, but I could write copy with my eyes closed. So I chose the easy option.

Many laughed when I told them I ran a copywriting agency, because I wasn't exactly the best speller in town. But at the time I didn't have anyone telling me the key to success is to do something you are passionate about. I just went with something that was easy, or so I thought.

A year passed and I couldn't break the £1,000 a month income. Social media was becoming more widely used, but businesses didn't know how to use it. I found it easy to pick up, so I studied it hard and shared my knowledge with others, and it wasn't long before I was tagged as the Social Media Queen. This was when I realised the power of having a Stage Name (I'll say more about this in the chapter on Hollywood Branding).

But again, although I was going round the whole of the southwest of England, teaching everyone and anyone how to use social media (from the Church of England Diocese to local radio stations and newspapers), I did not love what I was doing.

By 2012 I was desperate for money and still wasn't succeeding. Running my own business was looking like a dead end, and the security of a job was calling me. I knew that I had to stop running my business as a hobby and make a success of it.

I invested in a nine month growth accelerator programme where I finally went on a journey that helped me realise the mistakes I had been making in my business. And by the end of the nine month programme I was doing what I love. My business was flourishing and I was totally aligned with my passions and purpose. I have pivoted my business niche over the subsequent years, but the underlying teachings have been consistent: helping people launch businesses that they are passionate about.

Of course the journey didn't stop there. Running a business is a never-ending journey with dead ends, sheer cliff faces and huge mountains. But the important parts of the journey, that are relevant today, are the lessons I have learnt to date and which I share in this book.

LESSON: create a business you are passionate about.

Know your passion

I know beyond any doubt that my number one passion is creating businesses, closely followed by marketing and personal development. These three things make a killer combination and have been the catalyst for my success. You have to have passion for what you do; if you are even centimetre off course, the chances are you are going to fail.

I failed when I was an inch off course.

Instead of making the mistakes I made and waiting for your passion to find you, I suggest you actively go out and seek it. Passion is a strong and barely controllable emotion. You can find your passion by asking yourself some very simple questions:

- What could you happily do all day for free?
- What are you doing whenever you find yourself losing track of time?
- What do your family and friends say you love to do?
- What fills you up with excitement?
- What makes you laugh or makes you angry?

Go to my website if you'd like to take the Find Your Passions Challenge: www.amandacwatts.com/book-resources

Find your life's purpose

Having passion is important. But sometimes you will be unmotivated, tired and want to give up, even if you love what you do. Passion will not make you jump out of bed on these days. For this bed-ridden obstacle, you will need to find your purpose.

This one is a harder nut to crack, mainly because it is no longer all about you.

It is time to stop living life in your bubble. It may be safe and cosy, but now you have to step into the big, wide world to find your purpose.

Living in your bubble

When we live inside a bubble, we are concerned about our own pleasures and comfort. And we try not to be uncomfortable. This is why we might not exercise, or why we might have a takeaway Chinese on a Friday night.

The fear of being uncomfortable is also why we get anxious when we meet strangers or are in unfamiliar surroundings. This fear can often hamper our social and love lives.

Living inside our bubble keeps us small and makes us feel safe and secure. We discussed failure earlier... we rarely fail inside the bubble because we don't tackle anything to push us out of it.

Our bubble enables us to procrastinate. If we keep on doing what we have always done, we are safe.

In fact, pretty much all of our problems occur because we are living in a bubble, including the difficulty of living our life's purpose.

So if living in the bubble stops us from achieving greatness and success, what happens when we step outside the bubble and look outside ourselves?

Quite simply we see some amazing things.

Outside our bubble the world is no longer about us and our desires.

So when someone says something that upsets us, we have the opportunity to look from the outside in and see it's not really about us. It's about them: any fears, confusion or desire that they have.

When we step outside the bubble and look outwards we can see our purpose is actually about making the world a better place for others and future generations.

Once we get out of the bubble, see things with a wider view, we can create a new journey that becomes our life's purpose. We can start to see others, their suffering and their needs, and work towards making their lives better. We can then learn skills to help us become better at helping them. And as we go about our daily work we can ensure our actions are working towards our greater purpose.

And when we lose momentum for a while and our passion for our passion wanes slightly, we can step outside our bubble and feel motivated by the bigger purpose.

When you are regularly eating doughnuts, watching rubbish TV, procrastinating or fearful, you are in the bubble. When you can't stick to a healthy diet and are always reaching for the chocolate biscuits, you are in the bubble. These are signs you need to watch out for.

It is during these moments that you seek instant gratification and momentary pleasure. When you look from the outside in, you will see these actions for what they are: little desires and urges that can be let go.

But what matters most is becoming bigger than yourself. Once you do so, you will realise that you have a purpose in life.

Getting out of your bubble

When you realise you are in the bubble, expand your mind and your heart. See the bigger picture and look beyond the bubble.

Think about how others are feeling. Try and understand what they are going through, and rather than judge or condemn, understand instead. See that if others treat you badly it's not about you, but about them.

When you see the bigger picture it is genuinely easy to want others to be happy, just as you want your own happiness. A good way to stop feeling down is to do something for someone else. Mild depression can be eased by having a big purpose, and your purpose is found outside your bubble.

And when you step outside your bubble, you will see that there is a world out there that needs your help. You will have a gift and a way in which you can help others, be it through helping the planet, people's health and wellness, technology advancements, nutritional improvements or medicinal breakthroughs. Everyone has a purpose, and by actively searching for yours, you will find it.

The more you practise being there for others, the more you will learn that life is bigger than yourself. You'll learn that life is a gift that we have to share, and to make the most of it we must not waste a second of it.

There is nothing more fulfilling than having a purpose in life which will make the world a better place and the lives of those in it happier.

So I found my passion. And knowing it felt like the missing piece of the puzzle. That was until I got tired, or sick, or my children got sick and I had to take a day off. Then getting back into the saddle and keeping on going, no matter what, even when I wanted to stop, was hard.

There were weeks when I couldn't be bothered. There were days when I 'granted' myself a day off because the day before I had worked so hard. There were times when I would watch rubbish TV because I had lost my spark for the day.

I knew that my puzzle was still missing a piece. And it was only when I looked outside my bubble that I realised I needed to run my business for more than the sum of me. I needed to look and see what the big picture was rather than the day to day existence I was living.

The powerful me was almost there, but I was still not great.

Achieving Greatness

Greatness doesn't come from the busy work we do in life, which is exactly what I was doing: being busy while living my passion. Greatness comes from making a difference to the world.

Greatness comes when you set yourself an intention and choose to show up to that intention no matter what. It comes when you show up every single day.

Step one is to create a huge goal way outside of your comfort zone. And then use this goal to propel your mission. It becomes easy: head down, no procrastination, getting stuff done.

It's about doing what it takes, day in, day out, and achieving greatness. And it's about being relentless until you achieved it.

Greatness comes from finding passion and purpose. My purpose came when I looked outside my bubble. When I realised that being passionate and loving what you do in life is something that everyone should have the opportunity to do. So I created my mission: to help one million people out of employment to make following their passions their full time job. This is my purpose in life and why I jump out of bed every morning, excited to seize the day and make a meaningful difference to the world.

And, with the help of my wonderful team, I am well on the way to achieving it.

How are you going to achieve greatness? What can you do that is bigger than the sum of you; that will change people's lives for the better?

LESSON: create something that is more than the sum
of you.

The Conscious Competence Ladder

Awareness will change your life. Without awareness you cannot
make the right choices.

My wake-up moment was when I was crying in my parents'
bathroom. I saw that I was living my life in a certain way, and was
unconsciously incompetent when it came to the skill and awareness
of my choices and actions in life.

In case you are not familiar with this term, let me explain about the
Conscious Competence Ladder designed by Noel Burch.

It was developed to help us understand our thoughts and emotions
during a learning process. The model highlights two factors that
affect our thinking as we learn a new skill: consciousness (awareness)
and skill level (competence). According to the model, we move
through the following levels as we build competence in a new skill:

The four stages of learning any new skill

No matter what new skill we decide to learn, there are four stages
each of us goes though. Being aware of these stages helps us accept
that learning can be a frequently slow and uncomfortable process.
As you move from employee to business owner you will be learning
new sets of skills. You will have to think in a different way and take
action in ways you have never taken action before.

Let me talk you through the stages and how they relate to being an
entrepreneur.

Stage 1 – unconsciously incompetent. Some people will launch a business and maintain an 'I don't know what I don't know' state of existence. It will mean that their business will live in the land of doom. It will be an illusion, and they'll find it almost impossible to succeed.

It's very dangerous for FreedomPreneurs to be unconsciously incompetent. You will not be able to take your business to the next level.

Unfortunately, the reason so many businesses fail is because they don't realise they need to know more than they do. They believe they know everything already.

The solution: avoid this by surrounding yourself with trustworthy and wise mentors, coaches and advisors. Look where you want your business to go and make sure that you have someone who can help guide the way. If you have the right advisory network, you can avoid being unconsciously incompetent.

Consciously incompetent. This is only one step away from being unconsciously incompetent. I see many people using fear to keep them at this stage. Consciously incompetent is a FreedomPreneur who is struggling, knows why they are struggling, yet fails to do anything about it. I struggle the most when I see people in this stage.

I have trained many aspiring FreedomPreneurs, and it has been clear why they are not succeeding. Yet even knowing why they are struggling, they never do anything about it and therefore stay in the land of consciously incompetent.

The solution: if someone enables you to become conscious of a shortcoming or an area that needs working on (fixing), you need to do something about it. You need to take action on what the missing piece of the puzzle is and get competent. Believe me, you do not want to dwell in the land of consciously incompetent for long. It can lead to depression, frustration and anger. This is when you need to look outside of your bubble and find solutions.

Consciously competent. Becoming consciously competent is a highly rewarding time. This is where you start to celebrate the wins that you achieve as you have been building your weaknesses into strengths.

Being consciously competent is the mode that most moderately successful FreedomPreneurs operate in. They know what they need to know, and know how to achieve it. They make an effort to focus on the goals they need to achieve. And they do a pretty good job of it too.

The solution: note I said *moderately* successful. This is the minimum level of competence you must be at to have some success. Because you have mentors and advisors around you, you will learn what you need to do to overcome your weaknesses as they arise. You will naturally move into this state for most things you strive to achieve, but if you want to go from moderate to mastery then you need to aspire to level four.

Unconsciously competent. Some people are fortunate to be so good at what they do, they can do it in their sleep. This is mastery. You can call it the David Beckham stage – a star athlete who effortlessly excelled in his field of expertise.

Most successful FreedomPreneurs I have known combine their passions with their natural talents and 10,000 hours of mastery. If you become a FreedomPreneur at this stage then you are operating at an extremely high level of competence.

After understanding what it takes to be a FreedomPreneur, people such as Steve Jobs, Richard Branson and Warren Buffet became exceedingly successful.

The solution: you don't need a solution if you are unconsciously competent. However, if you disrupt the markets you are working in to innovate, you will not get the rug pulled out from under you. Aim higher, act more boldly and never rest on your laurels.

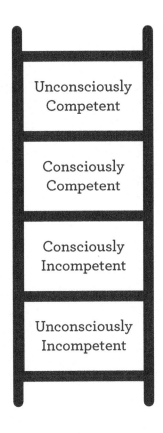

Unconsciously
Competent

Consciously
Competent

Consciously
Incompetent

Unconsciously
Incompetent

Gumption: Overcoming Fear

Where would you like to be five years from now? Do you want to be working in your day job, building someone else's dream, or aligning your passion with a *huge* purpose and achieving greatness?

Argh, if only it were as simple as that, right?

Having spent many years working with start-up enterprises, I know that what kept them from initially making the leap was one thing: fear. Fear of failure, fear of not making enough money and fear of people not liking what they have to say.

When I ask the question 'Where would you like to be in five years' time?' something often happens. Excuses happen.

'I would love to, but...'

'Yeah, but I can't do it because I have the children' or 'Yeah, but he succeeded because...It's not the same for me, I don't have time'.

Did excuses happen to you?

It's possible you have come up with reasons why you can't take action *now* and have to wait – wait until after Christmas because it's a busy time for the family. Wait until you are making a little more money so you can afford to save. Wait until the children leave home so that you can commit 100% to it. Wait until you have more clarity, because you are not sure how it will work.

I hate to be the one to break it to you, but this is just fear manifesting in excuses. This fear is stopping you from putting yourself into the world to be heard.

We all want perfection, but until we realise that the only way to get better, grow and learn is through failure, we spend our lives avoiding failure like our life depends on it. (It doesn't, by the way.)

To do, or not to do. To try, or not to try.

Most people live their lives thinking that if they say nothing and choose to take no action, they will avoid bad things happening to them. But this is the real kicker: if you choose to say nothing and do nothing, you are *more* likely to fail because you are not taking positive action to move forward with your life. If you are not growing, you are dying.

Confidence and fear

The opposite of living in fear is living with confidence. It's about confidently making decisions and confidently standing by those decisions.

We are born confident – but this confidence diminishes as we take on other people's opinions and make them our own. Our confidence can often turn into fear.

I have a fear of heights, as does my mother and my son. Do you think that we were born with this fear of heights? No even slightly. My fear is the result of my mother saying 'Be careful' and 'Don't get too near the edge' in certain situations. My son's fear of heights is from me saying the same thing to him. It is learnt behaviour.

Fear is not real. When we realise that fear is just a story we tell ourselves, we can consciously overcome it. And it all starts with one word: gumption.

Using gumption to give you confidence, no matter what

Gumption is 'the ability to decide what is the best thing to do in a particular situation and to do it with energy and determination.' (Cambridge Dictionaries Online) No matter what. Even if you are scared.

There will be certain times and situations when you will be scared or feel uncomfortable. There are certain times and situations when you *must* push outside your comfort zone, because that is where the magic happens.

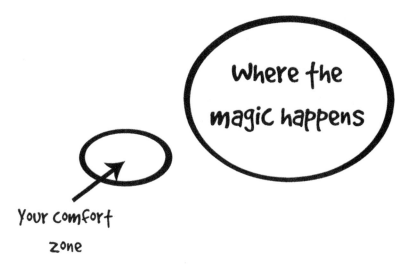

Where the magic happens

Your comfort zone

That is when you have to let gumption kick in. There will be times when you feel unconfident, scared and unsure. But your why will carry you through and gumption will kick in. Be courageous and know it is for the greater good.

As we progress up the Conscious Competence Ladder, our need for gumption gets less as we unconsciously take the right action.

Some of us will need less gumption than others. But we will all need it at times, do not kid yourself otherwise.

Please note: the more you believe in you, your product and services, the less gumption you will need. Confidence in your offering enables you to be more visible and step into more uncomfortable situations.

As you work through the modules in the book you will come across ideas that may push you out of your comfort zone. I may ask you to do things that you do not totally agree with and give you ideas that you have not used before. My advice is to get out of your own way and just do it! Don't live in fear and don't live in unconscious incompetence. Measure your results, and then let confidence grow as your business success grows.

If you keep on doing what you have always done, you will keep on getting what you have always got. Close your eyes and jump. It's going to be one hell of a ride!

There may be times when you find yourself going in a completely different direction to what you originally planned. Go with it and lean into the process. It works, so trust in it.

I have written this book to help you through the entrepreneurial journey, from unconscious incompetence to unconscious competence. I wish I had had it when I started on my journey.

However, having this book isn't going to guarantee you success. You must implement what you read and look for ways to break the mould and innovate. You are going to have good days and bad days, so the next stage is all about filling and fuelling.

Filling And Fuelling

There is no saying what is going to be in store for us on any given day. Life can throw curve balls and some days are going to be hard, but it's how you deal with them that will affect you in the long term.

The curve balls may be small inconveniences that test your patience, or may be a week-long sickness bug your children have that stops you from achieving anything.

The chances are you will create programmes and events that may not sell. You will have customers you didn't serve well enough. You will get people who hate what you stand for. You will want to give up. But you won't give up because you are going to be full and fuelled.

Let me explain.

Imagine a water bottle. If you took a quarter full water bottle and handed it to a small child, even though the child may be weak, they would easily be able to crush it. However, if this same bottle was filled to the brim with water and sealed, it would be more difficult to dent or crush. When the bottle is full and sealed, the pressure is pushing out and it is strong and resistant to anything pushing into it.

You need to imagine you are that water bottle. You need to ensure you are full, and that your focus cannot seep out of you.

The saying 'Only the strong will survive' is true. You do have to be strong to be a successful entrepreneur. You have to be full and fuelled.

Are you entering the world mentally, emotionally and physically almost empty? Are you easily crushable? Or are you full to the brim, powerful and able to withstand whatever is thrown at you? Now is the time to check in with yourself and start to master your emotions.

Your natural state of mind will make a huge difference to how you feel when life throws you curve balls. And it is this state of mind that separates the powerful and successful from the average.

Keep thinking about the imagery of the water bottle as you find fear creeping into your marketing and business activities. Make sure that you are full to the brim and at your most powerful at all times.

The following information will help you fill yourself up and keep you fuelled on the journey ahead of you.

Filling yourself up – automatically kick-starting the powerful you

I have to be honest with you, some days you may wake up and feel tired, frustrated, longing to laze in bed and drink more cups of tea or coffee. You are only human.

The days you will feel like this will be the days when you have not filled yourself up. It may be you have eaten badly, drunk too much the night before, not been focused on your why or not exercised enough. There may be many reasons. But it will happen.

So we need to give you some rocket fuel. This rocket fuel will enable you to jump out of bed with excitement. It will enable you to ignore the naysayers. It will enable you to work into the night. It will enable you to stop procrastinating and start creating your business.

Rocket fuel: writing and rewriting your goals, daily

To achieve success, you must set goals. When you set these goals, you must take the necessary steps to achieve them.

The only way to focus on your goals is to know them like the back of your hand. Which means you have to write and rewrite them daily.

The reason most goals fail is because they are written once (if at all) and then forgotten. Most people only write their goals yearly, which is why most people fail to achieve their dreams. You are going to get into the habit of writing them daily, no ifs, no buts.

Why write your goals daily? Quite simply, it will get you more focused, more driven and more hungry to achieve them.

If you write your goals once, you will forget about them. If you forget about them, you will have no fuel to get you out of bed and help you through the rough patches of being an entrepreneur. Writing your goals daily enables you to remind yourself every morning (or evening) what you are striving for. Knowing your goals will keep you focused. You will be more determined.

In the last module of this book I will give you a Freedom Accelerator programme. This is a way to plan your day and week strategically so that you stay on track and are constantly moving forward. When you reach this section you will have daily actions to complete. Until you become unconsciously competent at writing down your goals daily, I suggest you add 'goal writing' as one of your actions.

Here is the goal setting technique that I use.

Get a notebook or journal and keep it with you at all times.

Day one: write down your top ten goals.

Day two: write down your top ten goals without referring to your previous list.

Day three and every day thereafter: write down your top ten goals without referring to your previous lists.

Once you start writing your top ten goals daily, you must never stop.

The first day you write your goals you will have to give it some thought. It may even be difficult to find ten goals. The second day it will become easier, but remember not to refer to your previous list.

As the days go by your ten goals will change in order and priority. You may write a goal one day which will not appear the next day. Sometimes it may disappear altogether.

Each day you write down your ten goals, your definitions will get sharper. You will eventually find yourself writing down the same goals every day. The priority and order may change, but you will be crystal clear on your goals. After about thirty days you will be writing the same goals every day.

At about this time something remarkable will happen: you will ignite your rocket fuel. You will be powerful. Your work and personal life will begin to improve dramatically. You will be laser focused and more creative. Your progress rate will increase and everything you do will change in a very positive way.

How to write your goals

To get the most out of this exercise you need to write your goals in a certain way. They must be written in the present tense, as if already achieved.

Instead of saying, 'I will earn £100,000 in the next six months' you write 'I earn £100,000 per year'.

They must be positive goals. Instead of saying, 'I will quit smoking' you instead write 'I am a non-smoker'. Your command must be positive because your subconscious mind cannot process a negative command.

Begin each of your goals with phrases such as:
- I earn...
- I weigh...
- I achieve...
- I win...
- I drive...
- I live...
- I serve...

You get the picture? Positive, powerful, and personal.

To add real strength to your goals also write a deadline, for example: 'I earn an average of £10,000 per month by 31 December 2xxx'.

Even if you don't know when the goal is going to be achieved, you must give yourself a firm deadline. Make them big goals; don't think and play small.

When you begin writing your goals, you may have no idea how they will be accomplished. But knowing the how is not part of the exercise. The exercise is to get you laser focused on what you want.

It is to give you the much needed rocket fuel to be a successful entrepreneur.

You have most of the answers inside you already.

If you have an idea in your conscious mind, you can train your unconscious to kick in and give you the answers.

Multiply your success ten times! You can multiply the effectiveness of your goal setting by applying three actions to each of your goals. Doing this will program your subconscious mind and you will start to achieve miracles.

Example: I earn £100,000 per year.

Action 1: I plan every day in advance.

Action 2: I spend two hours a day on marketing.

Action 3: I only action one task at a time until completed.

At a certain point you will start to action the steps you need to take in order to achieve that goal, sometimes without even thinking about it. What do we call this? Unconscious competence!

LESSON: writing your goals keeps you focused
            and fuelled.

Who You Hang
Around With Matters

'You are the average of the five people
you spend the most time with.'

JIM ROHN

This relates to the law of averages, which is the theory that the result of any given situation will be the average of all outcomes.

This is important to remember, because as a FreedomPreneur you must know that in order to increase your wins, you also have to increase your losses.

Let me repeat that: in order for you to increase your wins, you have to increase your losses.

When it comes to relationships we are greatly influenced by those we surround ourselves with: the ones who are closest to us. They affect our self-esteem, our thoughts, decisions and actions. Even when striving to be our own person, we are more affected by others than we care to think.

We need people – whether they are co-founders of our business, mentors, coaches, friends, family and/or confidants. The people you surround yourself with must help bring out the best of you. If you are the best, most talented, most knowledgeable person in the room, you are less likely to be stretched or become better.

At this moment in life you may not be surrounded by the right people for the journey you are about to undertake. If you keep on surrounding yourself with the people you have always surrounded yourself with, you will keep on having the life you have always had, which won't work if you are wanting your life to change.

It is time to consciously change who you hang around with.

You are the sum of the five people you hang around with most

As a FreedomPreneur you need to spend time with people who are already where you want to be and are living the life you want to lead.

Let me explain. When you buy a house, you want to buy the worst house on the best street. The reason for this is simple: you can't change the street you live on, but you can change the interior and exterior of a house to add more value. You don't want to buy the best house on the worst street, because there is no way to increase the value of your house as it is already at its best, and the street will limit its value.

This is how I want you to think when you choose who you surround yourself with. You want to be the worst house on the best street.

You want to be the person who can be developed the most, learn the most and soak up all the knowledge of those surrounding you. You want to be in the best environment possible to enable you to become the best possible version of yourself.

How do you find successful people?

One way to surround yourself with the right people is to hang out where successful people are hanging out. Joining a mastermind group is a great way to do this.

However, as you are starting off in business this may be something that isn't feasible, so hang out online with the right people. Videos, books, audios – all of these things can bring experts and mentors into your home and enable you to learn and grow from them.

I had a steep learning curve when I started on my personal development road. I spent hours watching, listening and learning from the great, including Tony Robbins, Jim Rohn, Brian Tracy and Grant Cardone. I would not be where I am today if I hadn't spent time 'hanging out' with these guys online.

As I launched my business, these people were who I spent most of my time with. I had to say goodbye to the mums who wanted to drink tea all day while their children were at school. I had to stop speaking about work to my parents, and I had to stop going out and partying and drinking as much as it wasn't conducive to reaching my goals of being a success.

For many hours a day I hung out with millionaires and billionaires online. And as I and my business grew, I started to meet in person more millionaires and billionaires, and hang out with them in real life.

Make a list. Think about where you want to take your business and make a list of those who are already where you want to be. By creating this list, you are making a more conscious effort to spend time interacting with these people.

Build a powerful network. It has been shown that the people we surround ourselves with influence us in subtle ways. In his 1937 bestseller *Think & Grow Rich*, Napoleon Hill talks of mastermind groups.

Mastermind groups

A mastermind group is a group of smart people who meet weekly, monthly or daily to tackle challenges and problems together. These groups provide a place for you to lean on others, give advice and share connections. They are very much about peer-to-peer mentoring, and if you are lucky enough to get invited to one you will most likely see a marked change in your business, and yourself.

When you launch a new business it can be lonely and stressful. Belonging to a mastermind group means you will not feel alone when you are growing your business, which will dramatically improve your health and success.

A mastermind group will also enable you to expand your network. Your net worth equals your network (I will discuss this further in Part Two of the book). By joining a mastermind group, you typically add to your network, and gain the networks of those in the group with you.

LESSON: who you hang out with matters. Find people who are where you want to be, not people who are where you want to leave.

Create not consume

It's pretty addictive, learning from YouTube, reading motivational books, going to seminars, learning, learning, learning. Although this is something you must do, there does come a stage when you have to stop spending all your time learning and start creating your own information.

Creating your own information means embracing blogging, vlogging, webinars and running seminars, to name but a few. I must stress to you the importance of creating your own information and not just consuming others' work.

As you work on your personal development, spend time tapping into your unconscious and come up with your own ideas, programmes and blogs. You will be on a fast and exciting learning curve when you start a business, and it is easy to regurgitate other people's information rather than create your own thoughts on a subject. This brings us back to fear. When you're consuming other people's content, there is no risk to you. You will not be putting yourself outside of your comfort zone and letting your opinions and views be heard. By consuming, you continue to play small and put off making big statements that will draw attention.

But if you do not draw attention to yourself, you will continually be overlooked. Which is why you have to create content. Constantly innovate and share your thoughts and ideas so that people know what you stand for and want what you have got.

You can learn by burying yourself in a library, or you can learn by creating something outstanding.

Every time I write a blog I learn more. As I write this book I am learning. A blog, YouTube video or webinar means I have to tap into my knowledge and create new ideas and thoughts to help my clients and prospects. Each piece of content I create gives me the opportunity to provide untold value to the consumer.

Creating gives me ideas, experience and massive results. And it gives others the chance to learn.

At the beginning of your journey you will need to consume a lot, but what you really need to do to become good at something is to do it. It's not about learning as much as you can, but taking action as much as you can.

And if you can't do it, get others to help you. Outsource.

You will be faced with a create-or-consume dilemma every day. Your success will depend on your decision. Do I respond to emails or help a client? Do I read a blog post or write one? Do I listen to an audiobook or record my own podcast? Do I take another course or create my own life changing course?

You know the answer.

Create first, then if there is time afterwards, you can consume. If you feel like it. But creating gets addictive. The more courses, programmes, blogs, videos and audios you create, the deeper foundations your business will have. There will be someone out there who will happily pay for something that is stuck inside you, so delve deep and awaken the magic. You are doing a disservice to the world if you do not.

The sooner you start creating, the sooner you will make other people's lives better. And the sooner you make other people's lives better, the sooner you will have tangible results and experience. No amount of consuming will give you that.

LESSON: creating will give assets to your business. And income follows assets.

Take massive action

One thing that could really set you back with success is giving in to the fatal someday – 'Someday I'll write that blog'; 'Someday I will launch that new product'; 'Someday, someday'.

Someday never comes. Someday past by yesterday, and today you must take massive action.

This may well be one of the reasons you are stuck right now, either in a job when you want to launch your own business, or working in a business that is not bringing in the revenue. The likelihood is you are reading this book because something is missing.

As you go through the book, you will discover more and more strategies that will boost your chances of prosperity and wealth if you apply them to your start-up business.

You will learn many success principles on your journey to becoming a FreedomPreneur. But remember, success only comes to those who go out and grab it with both hands and work for it. Instead of adding this to the list of books you have consumed, why not take action on what you have read? There are worksheets to download from the website and strategies you can implement to catapult your success.

If you consume this book and create nothing, you will continue to get what you have always got. By taking massive action you will accelerate your journey. And don't worry about getting it 100% right and making sure everything is perfect. You don't have to get it right; you just have to take massive action. You can always go back and refine it later on, but for now just get it out there.

Nothing will happen until you take action, so let's dive into Part Two and create your dream business.

LESSON: 50% of something is better than 100% of nothing.
            Take action.

part two

The FreedomPreneur Methodology

The Five Step Method To Becoming A FreedomPreneur

1. Diamond Clarity
2. Hollywood Branding
3. Profit Packaging
4. Authentic Marketing
5. Wealth Breakthrough.

In every industry there is a person or business that stands out more than others, widely known for their expertise. They are the go-to people, products, services or businesses attracting untold opportunities that others can only wish for. Go-to people live a life of freedom and love what they do. They see their family more, have more holidays, live where they want to live, how they want to live.

The FreedomPreneur Method helps you step-by-step to become the go-to person in your niche industry. You will often hear me refer to it as becoming a Niche Celebrity.

If you have heard of the Pareto principle you will understand the 80/20 rule. It states 80% of the effects comes from 20% of the causes. The original observation was in connection with population and wealth. Pareto noticed that 80% of Italy's land was owned by 20% of the population.

He then carried out surveys on a variety of other countries and found to his surprise that a similar distribution applied. In 1992 a United Nations Development Program Report showed that the richest 20% of the worlds population controlled 82.7% of the worlds income.

If this rule works across all scenarios then in any industry the top 20% of businesses then control 80% of the wealth. They generate more revenue than the remaining 80%.

There are certain things you (and your business) need to have in place before even considering becoming a Niche Celebrity, and being part of the top 20% is one.

Now for those of you who are saying, 'Whoa, slow down, I don't want to earn fortunes', the UK Treasury revealed the top 10% earn an average of £60,500 a year in the UK, and the bottom 80% range from £8,600 a year through to £24,800. The figures paint a picture of what an average income is in the UK, and it may come as a surprise to you that an income of £39,800 will put you among the top 20% of earners.

Step 1: Diamond Clarity

Finding your business idea

In this chapter we are going to learn a simple but powerful strategy for finding a business that you want to run. If you already have a business, one of the reasons it may not have had the growth you desire or require is because you haven't found your business sweet-spot.

Many people believe that starting a business is a mysterious process. They think that their dreams will never be turned into a reality, and they don't know the first steps to take. In this chapter you're going to find out how to get a good idea for a start-up, and then throughout the rest of the book we will look at building foundations and strategies to keep your start-up staying-up.

But before we get started let's be clear on something: 99% of businesses fail. And the reason for this is because they never make it to market. Reasons people don't launch their businesses include:

Fear of failure. Many think starting a business is a big risk and it will be a failure. This fear can be caused by previous feelings of inadequacy, experiences of past failures in their lives and not wanting to replicate the feeling, and the real risk of starting a business – some will fail, but some won't. They may feel they are lacking in knowledge and are plagued by self-doubt.

> *'I have not failed, I've just found 10,000 ways that won't work.'*
> THOMAS A. EDDISON

*'I knew that if I failed I wouldn't regret that, but
I knew the one thing I might regret is not trying.'*
JEFF BEZOS, AMAZON FOUNDER AND CEO

Inadequate resources to start a business. Many have little or no money to start a business and they don't know where to find the capital to do so. They have no savings, no rich families or friends to borrow from and poor credit so they do not pass the bank's lending criteria.

However the UK is now a nation of bootstrapping entrepreneurs, with 49% of small business owners revealing they set up their business with under £2,000. And almost one in ten sets up their business with no funding needed whatsoever. This information is taken from the Entrepreneur Index, which crunches data from Companies House, Office of National Statistics and Experian.

I left school at the age of eighteen, and went straight to work in an admin department of a magazine company. I spent ten years climbing the ranks slowly and painfully to become a director of an exhibition. After leaving the corporate world for a short period to get married and have children, I found myself at a crossroads: to start my own business, or go back to the corporate jungle?

In 2009, after finding myself jobless, homeless and penniless I decided to start my business while I was a single mum on housing benefit. I had two children aged five and eight and literally started with a computer, spending my daytime meeting people and networking instead of watching TV.

It was by connecting with potential clients, joint venture partners and networking as much as I could when the children were at school that I eventually got off housing benefit and funded our lives through my business earnings. I started with nothing.

No exposure to entrepreneurship. Many have not been exposed to entrepreneurship and do not consider starting a business as an option for them. They may have hundreds of ideas, but they are just ideas. Many FreedomPreneurs come from an entrepreneurial background, with friends or relatives who inspire them to make the leap into the entrepreneurial world.

> *'Entrepreneur is someone who has a vision for something and a want to create.'*
>
> DAVID KARP, TUMBLR FOUNDER

Oprah Winfrey was born into a poor family in Mississippi, but this didn't stop her from winning a scholarship to Tennessee State University and becoming the first African American TV correspondent in Nashville at the age of nineteen.

In 1983, Winfrey moved to Chicago to work for an AM talk show which would later be called *The Oprah Winfrey Show.*

Poor view of people with money. Some don't view people with money, including business owners and entrepreneurs, positively. They think these people are greedy, unhappy, stressed and obsessed with making more money, so they don't want to be like them. They are sure money will change them and this stops them from launching their dream.

Luxury goods mogul François Pinault is now the face of fashion conglomerate Kering (formerly PPR), but in 1974 he had to quit high school because he was teased so harshly for being poor. As a businessman, Pinault is known for his 'predator' tactic, which included buying smaller firms for a fraction of their value when the market crashed. He eventually started PPR, which owns high-end fashion houses including Gucci, Stella McCartney, Alexander McQueen and Yves Saint Laurent.

Fear of selling. Whether you have a service-oriented business or are producing a product, being in business means selling. Unfortunately, there are many people who don't know how or even like to sell. They are intimidated by the whole process of selling, especially during negotiations. They don't think they have the gifts that excellent salesmen are supposed to have. They fear rejection, especially in terms of prospecting clients.

Need the security of a steady paycheque. Starting a business can be like a full contact sport: sometimes you're up and sometimes you get knocked down. This means that there might be days of plenty, but also days when cash flow is extremely tight. There are people who cannot live with the ups and downs of running a business, and instead prefer the stability and security of a job and a regular paycheque.

Ralph Lauren was once a clerk at Brooks Brothers. Lauren graduated from high school in the Bronx, NY, but later dropped out of college to join the Army. It was while working at Brooks Brothers that Lauren questioned whether men were ready for wider and brighter designs in ties. The year he decided to make his dream a reality, 1967, Lauren sold $500,000 worth of ties. He started Polo the next year.

Not driven to succeed. Some people have no big ambitions for themselves. They are content to live their lives peacefully, calmly, without any stress brought about by starting a business. They have no profit motive. And if money is a motivator, they feel that they can get it from their current jobs, working within an organisation instead of spearheading one.

Leonardo Del Vecchio grew up in an orphanage. One of five children, he was eventually sent to the orphanage because his widowed mother couldn't care for him. He would later work in a factory making moulds of auto parts and eyeglass frames where he lost part of his finger.

At the age of twenty-three, Del Vecchio opened his own moulding shop, which expanded to become the world's largest maker of sunglasses and prescription eyewear for brands like Ray-Ban and Oakley.

No idea what business to start. Even if a person likes the idea of starting a business, their next comment may be, 'But I do not know what business to start'. Deciding and determining what business to start is a huge stumbling block for many, which is where this chapter really will help you go from business idea to successful start-up.

Estimates vary, but more than 100,000 new ventures are created every year in the UK. Yet for every British citizen who actually starts a business, there are likely to be millions who begin each year saying 'OK, this year I am going to start my business', and then they don't.

Everyone has their roadblock, many of which I have already mentioned, but fear is the biggest thing that stops people from making this exciting leap. This is why so many people who come from a background with very little do make the leap and succeed. They have nothing to lose. The only way is up in their eyes.

Some believe that they have to come up with something new, something that isn't already invented, or a service that isn't already out there. In other words, they think they have to reinvent the wheel. But unless you are a technical genius, another Steve Jobs or Bill Gates, trying to reinvent the wheel is a big waste of time.

For most people starting a business, the issue should not be about coming up with something new that no one has ever heard of, but instead answering some very simple questions to find their business sweet-spot.

If you could create the perfect company, where would you begin? Would it be about the money, or about something you care about? How about something that you excel at and are really talented at?

Why choose? In fact you can have it all, and the most successful businesses do.

Your business sweet-spot is exactly the spot you want to be at when you set up your business and come up with an idea. It is about creating a vision for your business, and then taking action on it.

But how do you come up with a vision? Quite simply it's a combination of three things.

Your business sweet-spot

What are you passionate about? This is defined by three elements – your mission, your values and your interests. What lights you up inside, is something that you can do all day and love every minute of it? What makes your heart sing? On the opposite side of this, is there something you completely disagree with that makes you really angry? Something you want to change and know that this is your mission in life?

What are your talents? This is often defined by your 10,000 hours of mastery. In the book *Outliers*, author Malcolm Gladwell says that it takes roughly 10,000 hours of practice to achieve mastery in a field. What do you have 10,000 hours of experience in that you could use in your business? This is the one thing you are really good at and can do in a world-class manner.

What makes money? This is sadly where business ideas start and end, and why so many fail. People develop a business while chasing money, and when the going gets tough and they get knocked down, they give up. If you chase money you may be rich in pocket, but poor in life.

Your business sweet-spot is one of the most powerful (and profitable) ways to build the foundations of a successful business. But why?

Because you are being paid to do something you love; something that comes naturally to you; something you are great at. Because you are providing such an amazing service and solving your ideal clients' problems (more on that later), customers will rave about you. Your business will grow.

If you don't create your business in your sweet-spot then there are problems, as this diagram clearly shows.

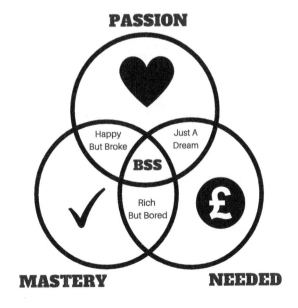

So let's break this down and either test your business idea or create a business idea.

Your natural skills and talents. What are you good at? What do people praise you for? Right now you may want to be modest, but try and stop that.

Your likes and passions. What do you love doing? What do you like doing so much that time passes without you realising?

Potential products and services and your paying client. Where is the overlap in your natural skills and talents and your likes and passions? How can you solve a problem in this overlap area and who would you solve this problem for?

People are happy to pay to have their problems solved. Almost every product or service involves solving a problem or filling a gap in a customer's life. Which group of people would have a problem in your ideal area? Is there a stand-out idea that fits your passions, skills, solves a pain point and has an audience willing and able to pay?

Going through this process will significantly narrow down your ideas.

Download the Business Idea Starter Kit Workbook here: www.amandacwatts.com/book-resources

Your target market, niche and ideal client

According to Bloomberg, eight out of ten small businesses fail in the first eighteen months.

There are many reasons why, but one of the main reasons is not because customers don't want what is being offered, but rather the business's target market and niche aren't clear, and it is trying to market to everyone.

You can validate your idea initially by completing the Business Idea Starter Kit. If you haven't already downloaded it, I'd recommend you do so now www.amandacwatts.com/book-resources. If you can't communicate clearly and specifically what you do and for whom, then your idea may sink like the Titanic.

Finding and choosing a niche

To find a niche that truly fits and that you are comfortable with, you need to start trading. As a new FreedomPreneur, finding your niche can be one of the most daunting things you need to do, so more often than not I recommend getting out into the marketplace and serving people. This is slightly more difficult when you create a product rather than a service because you need to build something, but you won't know whether your niche will work unless you try it.

However, when you are making this decision it is important to think about how you can niche. Here are two ways to set you off on the right path to finding a niche for your business.

Niche idea one: your niche is where you fit in. Finding a niche as an aspiring coach, web entrepreneur, app designer, florist or product developer is as important as remembering to take your skiing equipment with you when you visit Switzerland in the snowy season. If you don't, you won't get very far.

Your niche is not just your target market, it is also how you want to position yourself in the community, both online and out in the big, wide world. It is about where you would like to be most known.

When you are comfortable in your niche it feels like home. I often say your niche is like a pair of comfy slippers. You will try on many different kinds of footwear, but when you can easily glide into your niche and it feels warm, safe and the right fit, you have found the right one.

It is interesting to consider the origins of the word 'niche'. It comes from the 16th Century Middle French verb *nicher*, which means 'to make a nest'. In niching, you're making your own nest in the world that you can operate your greatest strengths and creativity from; somewhere that feels like home for you.

But remember, if there are places you fit, then that means there are places you don't fit as well. If one role is perfect for you, then other roles will not suit you, which is a tremendous relief. Now you know that you don't have to do everything and be everything.

The worst possible description of a chosen niche would be: 'I help people get from having problems to getting the results they want. I do it in any way at a time that they would like it done.'

Argh! I know someone who uses this description when he goes out networking face to face.

'I solve problems,' he says.

'What kind of problems?' people ask.

'What kind of problems do you have?' he says.

And then he goes on to tell them he solves those very problems. This may work face to face, but imagine how you would market this business. Quite honestly, you can't. And it is business suicide.

One of my favourite questions to ask my clients when they're trying to figure out their niche is, 'What's the perfect moment for you to enter your client's life?' After all, there will be a moment when it's too soon (the client is not ready for your help) and a moment when it's too late (they no longer need your help). Then there is a moment where you belong. There is a place where you belong. And because it is your place, it's important to be honest if you feel good about being there.

It's important to ask yourself, 'If I were at a party and overheard people talking about me and how I'm the go-to person for _____ , would I be happy or sad about that?'

Depending on your answer, you may have already found your niche.

Niche idea two: filling the gap. Having a niche that fills a gap in the world is a great way to dominate your chosen marketplace. If you have something that will never be in the world if you don't put it out there, then you have found a gap in the market that may need filling. If you fill it, the whole community may be stronger for it. Or it may be something that is already there but you do it in a totally unique way. For example massage, but done in a way never experienced before.

Creating a way of doing something that is unique to you is easier than you think when you create a service product. We cover more of this and creating a signature system in the 'Profit Packaging' section.

I find invariably when I meet someone with a great niche and ask them where it came from, they tell me it was from some part of them noticing that no one else was doing something. After wishing they could have found something somewhere else, they decided to do it themselves.

A niche is inevitable. Either you choose it or the world chooses it for you. You cannot not have a niche. Every business out there has a niche – it's where you fit in the marketplace. There will always be a role you are playing that others don't play, whether this is a conscious or unconscious decision.

The only question is – are you playing the role you want to play? You might be known as a generalist who is good at a lot of things – and it's easy to forget that a generalist is still niche as it's how you will be known in the wider community. Others may be specialists who are really good and focus on one thing. In our culture specialists are more valued financially, which is why having a specific niche is recommended when setting up your business.

Whether we choose our niche or not, we will all be known for something. We will be pigeonholed into roles. We are pigeonholed in our personal lives (I'm the spontaneous one, my sister is the tidy one). We are pigeonholed in our careers (I was the Director of Ideas, another director was the Sales Expert). We are pigeonholed in our relationships (I am the bossy one, apparently!). Joking aside, we are all labelled. It is our responsibility in our business to make sure we are labelled as we want to be.

A good question to ask yourself is, 'What roles am I stuck in that I don't want to be stuck in anymore?' And then ask yourself what you'd like instead.

A niche is inevitable.

The four steps to niching

What? What is the missing piece of the puzzle? What is something that's missing in your community or marketplace; something that you don't see being offered?

Why? You may have noticed the missing piece of the puzzle whereas others may not. Your experiences will have determined why you saw this gap in the market and shaped your need to fill it. Your story (more on this in 'Hollywood Branding') will have a lot to do with why you are drawn to a certain gap.

How? How are you going to go about the work that you do for your niche? If your business was a plane that took people from London to New York, there might be many routes it could take, but your niche is the route you decide to take. Your niche isn't just about deciding on what you want to offer, but also on how you want to offer it. If people say, 'Why should I work with you?' or 'What is different about what you do?', having your niche enables you to know confidently what makes you different. It's the old fashioned USP (unique selling proposition). This is your how.

Who? This is your Perfect Fit: the person who represents your ideal client. It is crucial to identify your Perfect Fit in your business, and it's vital to your marketing so that you can see if a client is really fit to work with you or not.

When we first start out, we often want to work with anyone. But soon we realise that this doesn't work for us. We realise that we have standards, and we cannot put ourselves last when running a business. We want people who show up to their appointments on time, or if they have to cancel last minute, pay for them. We want people who are willing to do the homework we give them; people who are appreciative of our work. And as our own map becomes clearer, we realise that we need to work with people who share our fundamental point of view.

The Perfect Fit

The Perfect Fit is otherwise known as a customer profile, ideal customer or customer avatar.

In other words, it is the person who will get the most out of working with you; the person who will benefit the most, be the happiest customer, and gladly evangelise your virtues to the world. Figuring out who this person is – figuring out whom you want and need to be serving – is an exercise in customer profiling.

At its simplest, figure out who you want to do business with (the Perfect Fit) and what makes them tick so they will do business with you.

When starting a business, knowing whom you want to sell to is more important than what you want to sell. Even if you already have a product in mind, identifying your target market is key to your new business's success.

In this section I am going to walk you through the steps to identifying your Perfect Fit, and we will use this as a foundation for your business so you become a FreedomPreneur.

Why you need to start with your target market and find your Perfect Fit. Starting with your product rather than the people you want to serve is like putting the cart before the horse. If you think about your ideal target market, then you can create your ideal product/service with them in mind and have your Perfect Fit.

If you create your product first and then search high and low to find a person who might need it and pay for it, you are setting yourself up for falling at the first hurdle. You might find yourself trying to make a client fit to your idea and this is what I call a phantom client (they don't really exist).

Knowing your ideal client first is a far more effective and stable way to launch a new product or business.

If you are like most FreedomPreneurs, your desire to have a business either started with an idea or a problem that you wanted to solve. This is the perfect way to think about your business – I speak of it as a necessity in the 'Business Sweet-Spot' section – but it isn't the best way to launch your business. In fact, the reason I have written this book is to ensure you don't fail in the first year, and forgetting the first step ('Diamond Clarity') is why so many businesses do go under. If you let the excitement of launching your business take over before you are ready and put the cart before the horse, you will spend far more time spinning wheels and getting nowhere than if you do your homework diligently and delve deep into understanding your ideal client.

We have discussed your business sweet-spot. Now you need to take a step back and think about the people you want to serve, not what you are going to offer.

Here are a few reasons why defining your target market should be uppermost in your mind before you launch your business:

1. Finding a core group of people and solving their existing problem is far easier than designing a product or service from scratch that you want, but nobody else does

2. You can validate your offer quickly and go from zero to a healthy income in less than one month. This means that you take less risks and are quicker in getting your start-up to stay up

3. You are focusing on helping people instead of selling a product you want to sell. This means you develop a lifelong relationship with your audience. They become your core customers, and you can sell to them time and time again

4. Knowing your target market will ensure that you shape your branding according to your client, not based on what you want to have on your website

5. Understanding your client will make finding images easier as you will know what to look for and what will appeal to your ideal client

6. Knowing your client will make it easy for you to have clarity on what kind of service packages or products you need to create for them, and will ensure that you will create what they actually need rather than what you think they might need.

Common mistakes to avoid. Starting with your target market is easier than the 'products first' approach, but you still have to make sure you don't make these common mistakes:

Don't look for markets with no competition. If you are wanting to work in a space with no competition then the chances are there isn't a market for your product, or there is little money in the space. Ideally you want fierce but incompetent competition. It is actually relatively easy to own your space and dominate the marketplace, mainly because 99% of the competition is rather abysmal.

Don't try and appeal to everyone. It is important to niche your target market. If you appeal to everyone, you appeal to no one. I had a friend who wanted to work with women in the corporate and business owner sector, helping them to become successful leaders. The problem she encountered time and time again was that she was trying to appeal to two different markets.

Being a leader of a team in the corporate world is very different from being a leader in your own business. Her message fell on deaf ears; she couldn't find regular clients who resonated with it. I believed it was fear stopping her from choosing a niche, but in fact it was fear of niching that was stopping her from becoming a Niche Celebrity and getting clients with ease.

Have you heard the saying: If you chase two rabbits at the same time, you catch neither.

Don't create a phantom market. Yes, believe it or not it is possible to create a market that doesn't exist. If you are already excited about the product you want to sell, you may be tempted to create a market around it. The problem with this is you may be creating a phantom market, which is why it is better to focus on the problem you want to solve instead of the solution you want to offer. Have your target market in mind first.

What constitutes the Perfect Fit? First of all we need to remember we are creating a business for you as well as helping your Perfect Fit, so here is a breakdown of what constitutes a Perfect Fit:

- Those you really enjoy working with
- Those who need your help, badly
- Those who recognise that working with you is essential
- Those who can easily be identified and contacted
- Those who will happily pay what you're worth, without negotiating
- Those who will get great results from working with you (and write testimonials to prove it)
- Those who will tell others about you and refer other clients over and over again.

And if you are really honest with yourself, these are the only kinds of people you want to work with. But to get a business full of these kind of clients you need to stop marketing to everyone and anyone and start marketing to a specific audience.

This section of the book will help you do that.

How to find your Perfect Fit. Finding your Perfect Fit, niche and product is an exciting step in creating your freedom business. Once you know your Perfect Fit, they need to be part of your life and your number one priority when you create any kind of marketing strategy.

It is important to be highly specific; way more specific than you probably feel is necessary. No detail is too minor.

Once you have your Perfect Fit customer profile, you can start to create your offering to speak directly to them. You will have Diamond Clarity and deep foundations for growing your freedom-based business.

This is *huge* in terms of the marketing and campaigns you will run in the future, and you will save lots of money that might otherwise be wasted on campaigns appealing to no one.

The other thing you need to be aware of is the Perfect Fit is not a generic 'target customer' profile where you might say your ideal client is a forty-five to fifty-five-year-old lady, middle class, who lives in the countryside. For the Perfect Fit ideal client, that won't cut it. We don't use ranges and we don't skip details.

If you really want to delve deep, go to my website and download the 50 Questions you need to answer to create the Perfect Fit Profile Workbook. Tons of FreedomPreneurs skim over this work when they're starting a business, and it always shows in the end. www.amandacwatts.com/book-resources

Having a rigorously detailed profile has countless benefits. Knowing specific details about the person you are targeting results in stronger messaging and knowing where to do your marketing.

When you write an email, blog post or sales letter as though you are addressing your Perfect Fit, your message will resonate – loudly (even with people who aren't your Perfect Fit).

Starting a relationship on this positive footing means you can quickly build up to becoming an authority and will see a much shorter sales cycle. New customers inevitably mean referrals, new friends and colleagues, and new ideas.

The long and short of it is that if you don't have a well-crafted, highly detailed customer profile, most of what you're doing is going to be guesswork.

It is very common for FreedomPreneurs (new and seasoned) to be totally convinced that they know who they're going after, but when you ask them to write it down, suddenly they have nothing real to say about the person they want to serve. They have been working on hunches and guesswork that have never been validated.

A detailed client profile will protect you from going down many of the wrong paths, so please take the time to sit down and think through who your Perfect Fit is likely to be and where they're likely to go. After going to the website and downloading and completing the workbook, you can then craft your ideal client profile.

Client profiles

First of all you need to give the Perfect Fit a name. Once you have a name for your Perfect Fit client, you then need to write out in detail:

Who they are. This is where you think about what they currently do, what their personality is and what they are looking for.

What their challenges tend to be. This is where you delve into their current challenges and really understand what is stopping them from reaching the goals they want to achieve.

What is the one thing they need right now? This is where you look at overcoming the challenges that they are having and provide options for them to buy from you.

Whether you are selling a product or service, knowing your customer in depth will determine how successful your creation is.

You will need to answer the questions in the Perfect Fit Profile Workbook to be able to complete this section fully. Some of the questions in the workbook include: what does your client want? (Make sure that you use their feelings and their words.) What keeps them up at night? (Picture them, tossing and turning at 3am, worried or scared about something.) What are their top three daily frustrations?

1.

2.

3.

What would they do anything, pay anything, to solve/get rid of/achieve?

1.

2.

3.

4.

5.

It is with these and many other questions that you will really get to know your ideal client. From these you can create your Perfect Fit. And by creating your Perfect Fit, you can create powerful sales and marketing strategies and build your business to become a FreedomPreneur.

Let me give you an example of the Perfect Fit profile from one of my coaching programmes, and a Perfect Fit profile that one of my clients created for her Perfect Fit.

Client Profile 1 – Frustrated Fraser

Who is he? Frustrated Fraser is stressed, bored and fed up in his corporate job and he wants to make the leap and set up his own business.

He is currently dreaming of ideas to enable him to leave his job, having decided that this is what he wants to do. He needs a step by step plan to help him leave with confidence and create a start-up business that stays up. His dream is to replace his corporate salary with doing what he loves in his own business and having a better lifestyle. He wants freedom.

He needs to become Making-the-leap Matthew.

Making-the-leap Matthew is a high performing professional corporate employee in his thirties–fifties. He is smart, highly motivated and looking to transition from a lacklustre job to a business he loves. He is fed up with the dark winter mornings and the long commute. He works long hours and doesn't have the life he really wants. He wants to spend more time with his family, or make time to have a family. He wants to have more fun and excitement in his life and start living again.

What Making-the-leap Matthew's challenges tend to be:
he's super passionate about making the leap and transitioning into having his own business. In fact, he knows that this is his calling. He understands that it is time to stop building someone else's dreams and build his own instead. He so badly wants to change his life, but right now he doesn't have any idea how to set up a business and start to attract clients. He is not close to understanding the modern digital marketing, and although he is an extremely high performer, he doesn't know what he needs to focus on to go from business idea to FreedomPreneur.

But this is because he doesn't know what he doesn't know about running his own business. He needs to learn what it takes to ensure that he doesn't lose money and make unnecessary mistakes. Which of course will lead him back to a day job. He is very excited about the possibilities, but until now they have just been dreams inside his head with no plan. He knows he can't keep working for the corporation he currently works for, but he feels overwhelmed at the thought of going it alone and having uncertain paydays.

If he is really honest, he has a little self-doubt and wonders if he is actually cut out to have his own business and be successful in his own right.

What he needs right now: his primary focus needs to be on having deep foundations to his business and diamond clarity on his ideal clients, where to find them, and the services he is offering. It is all about finding his business sweet-spot, getting his marketing material in place and getting his product and service to market.

It is important that he gets his marketing message right so that he can fill his pipeline quickly and turn prospects into paying clients while putting his marketing on autopilot. At the same time it is important he looks at his products and programmes, especially his pricing. Then it is about stating specific goals and creating focus and accountability to move his business from start-up to FreedomPreneur.

By writing out the client profile in such detail, you make it clear whom you help, and how you help them. By writing a client profile and designing your Perfect Fit, you can ensure that you speak to your ideal clients throughout all of your marketing.

Client Profile 2 – Back-pain Becky

Who is she? Back-pain Becky is constantly in pain, avoiding being physically active as much as she can, and she has gradually put on weight as a result. She wishes she could do things she is passionate about and move again without fear of pain.

Although she was told there is no structural damage to her back and it's alright for her to resume her regular routine and exercise, she is afraid being more physically active will make her condition worse.

She spends thousands of pounds on therapies, but the results are short term. She doesn't feel motivated to continue the exercises the therapists advised her to do, and because she is not making progress, her pain comes back and gets worse.

Back-pain Becky is a high-performing professional corporate employee or entrepreneur. She is smart, highly motivated and looking to learn more about her body and establish strong, lasting foundations for health and physical movement which will help her reduce and eliminate her lower back pain.

She spends long hours sitting working and has little or no time set aside for herself. She wants and needs that time.

She is fed up with being in pain when she moves around and fearful she will have to live with it for the rest of her life. Living with pain for so long has affected her not only physically but also emotionally, mentally and socially. She feels depressed and doesn't want to do anything anymore.

She wishes she understood her condition and why bed rest is not the solution. She wants clarity on the methods of exercising, types of exercises she should do, and how they will make a difference in her life.

What are her challenges? Back-pain Becky wants to solve her lower back pain and go back to doing the things she loves; go back to her normal life. But at the moment she is struggling to get any results.

She doesn't want superficial results; she wants lasting foundations that will allow her to build a strong and balanced structure for the years to come. But she is not close to understanding her body, how it functions and what it needs. She also struggles to have a simple and straightforward lifestyle and a controlled, flexible diet she can shape to fit her busy life.

She wants to exercise in a correct way to ensure she doesn't make her condition worse, but she is unsure of where to start and how to keep herself motivated. She knows there is more to life and she wants to live it without fear of pain.

What does she need right now? What Back-pain Becky needs right now is to get her life back. Her primary focus needs to be reducing her lower back pain to the point where she can live her normal life again, so her first mission is to master body movement and set deep, lasting foundations. Those strong foundations need to be developed from correct physical movement patterns and she needs to strengthen her body from within, tackling the root cause of her pain. There is no room for superficial techniques or results. She needs a step-by-step process which makes sense and will not overwhelm her. Only then will she be able to build a strong, pain-free structure.

It is important to get her body mechanics right from the beginning, because how she uses her body will have a direct impact on her condition and subsequently her entire life. At the same time it is essential to fuel her body and mind with the right nutrients, not through a strict diet, but through a controlled diet. A diet is not something she goes on; it's something she can change and improve.

She needs someone qualified to work with her condition: a professional who has experience and has had results with others who have suffered just like her. As a high performing professional she wants to see results in numbers as her condition improves. She wants real assessments.

Then it is all about being consistent and practising the art of mastering her body and fuelling it the right way. Everything else will follow if she is consistent with her newly formed habits.

So now you can start to create your niche and your Perfect Fit. Once you have an idea on whom you want to serve, you need to see if you can find them easily online and offline.

Places to look include: online forums, conferences, blogging platforms, Facebook groups, LinkedIn groups, networking events and restaurants.

I will cover what to say and do once you are in front of your ideal clients in the 'Authentic Marketing' section, but for now you just have to make sure that they can be found online and offline and that you can market to them.

If you have no idea where you can find your ideal client then you need to do some research. And the best person to ask is your Perfect Fit.

Important points to take away for Diamond Clarity:

- Choose a niche or you will have one chosen for you. A niche is where you fit in or a gap in the market
- Know your what, why, how and who when choosing your niche
- Research your Perfect Fit
- Don't create a phantom market
- Create your Perfect Fit profile. You need to know your ideal client better than you know yourself.

Step 2: Hollywood Branding

Introduction to branding

Let's get to the point, fast! Your brand is not your logo. It is not the colours you want to use on your website and it certainly isn't the design on your business card. Your brand is so much more than all of these things.

Why call it Hollywood Branding? One thing I teach you in the next chapter ('Profit Packaging') is how to create a signature system that you will get known for. The FreedomPreneur Method is my signature system and Hollywood Branding is the second module in this system.

It was my easiest module to name because I was crystal clear about what branding can do for a business. Good branding attracts clients – a lot of clients! In fact, it can attract clients like paparazzi round a celebrity. Hence the name 'Hollywood Branding'.

And just like a celebrity, you can craft your brand so that you stand out from the crowd and elevate your image in the public eye. Hollywood Branding will ensure you are not seen as magnolia or vanilla (because no one really wants to be magnolia) but an altogether more exciting brand. To put it simply, Hollywood branding takes you from bland to brand.

Why brand your business? Branding is one of the most important aspects of any business, large or small, B2B (Business to Business) or retail. Creating an effective brand will give you a major edge in increasing competitive markets.

> *'In order to be irreplaceable one
> must always be different.'*
> COCO CHANEL

Whether you want to be a window cleaner, solicitor or run a restaurant, you need to create a Hollywood Brand. To make it a bit clearer, if you haven't already, you can replace the word branding with the word reputation.

When branding is done correctly, it should do two jobs: it should convey what is special about you and your business, and it should show you in a positive light.

Creating a small business means that often you gain a good reputation without having to give it much thought. When you are small it is easy to give and manage customer service. But imagine how powerful and successful your business would be if you gave a good impression all the time, even before your clients became clients. How much new business could you get then?

By following all the steps in 'Hollywood Branding' you will be well on your way to creating a strong and powerful brand. And who wouldn't want that, eh? So let's dive on in and create your brand.

The big mistake. The first thing most excited new FreedomPreneurs think of doing when given the task of creating a brand for their business is spending hours trawling the internet to see what their competitors are doing. This can immediately halt them in their tracks and send them running straight back to their day job because fear overtakes them and they think that they cannot do what others are doing.

The reason for this is because something horrible happens when people try and create a brand by looking at other businesses and competitors. They start to suffer with competitor-itis.

I am hoping that you haven't yet started researching and having the symptoms of competitor-itis, because this book is the vaccine you need to make sure you never suffer with the disease. Although knowing your competitors is something that you need to touch on briefly when creating your business, it is all too easy to obsess over what they are doing. This obsession may cause you to question your business, your idea, and sometimes even yourself.

Here are the reasons not to focus on competitors:

1. You lose focus if you obsess over the competition. If you take your eyes off your goals, you slow yourself down. It's like when someone interrupts your train of thought. It can take ages to get back to where you were, and your vision is not as clear as it was.

Just keep looking at your goals and keep working towards them. Do not lose focus.

2. You begin to second-guess yourself. When you have competitor-itis and are looking at what others do, it does nothing but raise questions in your mind. 'I wonder if I should be doing that?' and 'What would happen if...?' When you make unplanned changes you risk confusing your clients and your tribe (I know this from experience; competitor-itis was something I really suffered with when I started my business). And don't get me started on how confused *you* will end up. You'll lose your power and become weak.

3. You will always be one step behind your competition. The problem with watching someone else is that it puts them in the position of the leader and you are the follower, which is pretty accurate. I spent too much time watching big online business coaches and not carving my own path. I was becoming a smaller, less effective version of my competitors, and I was not being authentic. I was playing a waiting game, unable to work out what to do next. This was because I was waiting for my competitors to do their next thing so I could then do it myself.

Now my business model is *very* different from my competitors' business models as I have realised that to achieve success, I need to disrupt the industry, not follow it. As the majority of my competitors are looking for passive income creating online training programmes, I am one of a tiny handful in London that teaches full business training programmes over six months, live, in person.

4. You waste your time and creativity. Why do you think there are so many copycats out there? When you are looking at someone else and looking for the secret to their success, you are not creating new ideas. All you can do is what they are doing (as I said in the point above). You squash your creativity because you do not let your unique genius and brilliance out; you are just trying to emulate your competitors' brilliance, which of course you can't.

5. You consume rather than create. One of my mentors taught me a valuable lesson about consuming too much content. We covered this in the first section of the book, and we will cover it again in 'Authentic Marketing'. I cannot stress enough how important it is for you to create rather than consume. Personal development is very important for your success, but when you find yourself obsessing over others people's blogs, videos and podcasts, you just consume more and more and do not create anything for your business.

In fact, the more you create your own blogs, videos and audios, the more you will position yourself in the marketplace as a leader/expert. By sharing your thoughts on your chosen niche and the problems you help overcome, you get more clarity, and it soon becomes clear how different you are from your competitors. The moment you realise how different you are is the moment you can create a unique brand.

From the points above you can see clearly why you must not obsess over the competition. Instead create a Hollywood Brand using the five steps we are going to walk through together. Do not skip any of the steps, for within them lies the secret sauce to a Hollywood Brand.

If you need one more reason to work on this section in depth, remember that if you don't shape your brand, others will do it for you.

Brand position

The brand position is the part of the brand that describes:

- What your organisation does
- For whom you do it
- Benefits to your customer
- What makes you different from your competition (don't obsess).

Your brand positioning statement is the way you position your brand in the mind of your customers. Your positioning will be based on how you articulate and demonstrate your identity so that you own your niche.

You will already have done a lot of the much needed hard work and research in 'Diamond Clarity'. Your brand position may be about your company, or it may be about you. Will you or your business be the brand?

If you are your brand then you will create a positioning statement for you, and this will be the first step you take towards becoming a Niche Celebrity. This is not an either/or moment. You can create two brand positioning statements: one for you as the Niche Celebrity, and one for the business as the go-to business in your niche.

If your business is your brand and it doesn't have a 'figurehead' who is used for marketing purposes (a Niche Celebrity), then your positioning statement will be for your company alone. Having a strong leader whom customers and clients can admire, respect and look up to, like Apple, Virgin and Microsoft, will only enhance your brand.

Please do not skip this fundamental part of the foundations you are building as the information we create will be used in 'Authentic Marketing'.

Creating your brand positioning. Your product or service will be one in 7.4 billion. Why? Because you are unique. We have to answer the question 'With so many products/services, why should the customer choose mine?'

Positioning answers this question. A products/services position is the place that occupies the customer's mind. All products have a position, even if the position is unfamiliar or irrelevant. You even have a position if you are not very good. There is no escaping it, which is why *you* have to craft your positioning in the market, and deliver.

Successful products and services stand out. The purpose of positioning is to articulate what makes your product unique. And to articulate it we need to write the positioning statement.

A succinct positioning statement could be articulated as: 'Our (your offering) is the only (niche category) that (insert benefits)'.

Good positioning statements reflect good positioning. Thus the million dollar question is 'What is good positioning?'

1. Unique. Your positioning must be unique. To be really successful it must not already be owned by another company. If it is owned by another company, your mission is to get to top position, fast. It is very difficult to be the best if someone else is already the best. If there is already someone owning the space you want to be the best in, then you need to find a new angle. This is why a niche is so important. If you can't find a new angle, you will have to hustle like fury and become first in the space – I mean first in the clients' minds. But this is no easy task.

My advice: be unique.

Case study – Coca Cola and Pepsi

Pepsi has created a new soft drink and wants to position it as the world's number one soft drink. Unfortunately, Coca-Cola already owns this position in the mind of customers. Knocking Coca-Cola from that position is impossible. Pepsi can't do it. Coca-Cola own their niche, so Pepsi has to find another angle and niche to own.

How does it do this? It finds an open space: what do customers drink if they don't want Coke? Then instead of positioning its new drink as the best alternative to Coke, Pepsi positions it as the opposite.

This is the story of 7Up. Pepsi positioned it as the uncola. 'There is no cola like the uncola' was the slogan.

Case study – Apple and IBM

And then there is the most famous positioning we all know and love. In 1984 a new computer was invented. The inventor of this computer, Apple, decided they were not even going to try and knock the market leader IBM off its number one positioning as the computer for business people. Instead Apple repositioned the IBM PC as the square, boring and hard to use computer for people who like accounting. In contrast, Apple then positioned their invention as an easy to use computer for creative people who want to have fun.

Say hello to Macintosh.

And today, IBM doesn't make PCs anymore. HP and Dell are the leaders of PCs. And a Mac is still the easy to use, fun, stylish and cool alternative to the PC.

2. Think inch wide, mile deep. If your positioning is too broad, the customer won't remember it. If you are everything to everyone, you are nothing to anyone.

Consider the journey of Levi's. I remember when I was growing up in the late eighties and early nineties, the only denim to be seen in was Levi's. They were the leader even though a pair of Levi's jeans was not cheap, especially for a teenager who was still at college.

The reason the Levi company was so successful was because of its few successful styles. They didn't try to be all jeans to all people; they just had a few perfect pairs, the most successful being Levi 501s, and then arrived 505s and 517s.

But this all changed when Levi branched out and decided to introduce more styles. It now has a confusing array of products ranging from cheap to expensive, including shirts, skirts, hats and scarves. They make everything for everyone and the Levi's brand has lost its meaning.

Levi's went from being an iconic brand with iconic adverts and marketing in the eighties to a nothing brand. In fact, the Levi's adverts were so powerful that the soundtracks in them became hit songs again – think Sam Cooke, 'Wonderful World' (1986); 'The Joker', Steve Miller Band (1990); and 'Should I Stay Or Should I Go', The Clash (1991). Unfortunately by 2004 the Levi's adverts were no longer something we loved; the company's product strategy was now so confused and disorganised that it couldn't even make a good ad campaign. When it diversified from its niche, it lost its tribe. Is Levi still the leader in denim? Nope!

3. Affordable. Your budget will determine how narrow your positioning must be. Can you afford to be the best in the world, or do you need to be the best in your current location?

If you don't have millions for an advertising budget then think of something smaller. How about San Francisco? That is how Craigslist started and it grew from there, subsequently becoming the best online classifieds in the world.

You are creating a business, not a flash in the pan. It is a journey.

4. Strong. Good positioning is strong and unwavering in a customer's mind. But it must also be strong in your mind. Once your brand owns a position in your customers' minds, you are stuck with it.

Let's look at some Hollywood Brands and how they are positioned in our minds:

- Did you know that Xerox made a personal computer before Apple?
- Do you think of sandwiches when you think of Starbucks?
- Did you know that Kleenex makes paper towels?

Quite possibly not, because each of these brands is already positioned in your mind:

- Xerox = copiers
- Starbucks = coffee
- Kleenex = tissues.

It is very difficult to change a position you own, and in fact once you own a position you really don't want to change it. You want to keep it and grow your market share. You will be 'stuck' with your strong positioning for a long time, and this is a good thing – if you deliver.

As you think about your positioning, make sure you are happy with it, because once you have it, you will find it hard to shake.

5. Believable. To be believable you must deliver on your positioning promise, otherwise you will leave a gap in the market for others to own.

What if the first Mac had actually been boring and difficult to use? Then the positioning wouldn't have been believable and would have left a gap in the market.

Positioning your product/service. Now you understand the importance of positioning you can start to work on how you are going to position your business. Ask yourself these three questions:

1. Who are you? Are you a manufacturer? A service provider? A retailer?
2. What do you do? Do you make (insert product/service)? Do you fix (insert product/service)? Do you sell (insert product/service)?
3. Why does it matter? Are you the best? Are you the fastest? Are you the cheapest?

If you cannot answer these questions and brand position your own business, how will your clients be able to do so?

Brand promise

Your brand promise is the single most important thing that your organisation promises to deliver to your customers every time.

To come up with your brand promise, consider what customers, suppliers, employees and partners can expect from every interaction with you. What is it that you promise to deliver, time in, time out?

Think of your favourite brand. What does it deliver to you? The brand promise you create for your business has to be so solid that your clients develop expectations of your brand and trust you because they know you will deliver these expectations.

Danger: breaking the brand promise. When a brand fails to keep its brand promise, clients become confused and dissatisfied. It is difficult for a client to understand why their expectations aren't being met, and your reputation is tarnished. The knock on effect will be that your clients are likely to look for a replacement brand that does meet their expectations and keep its promise in every interaction.

Keeping the brand promise. Brands that keep their brand promise throughout their business (this includes internal promise, client promise and marketing promise) are very powerful. When clients trust that a brand will meet their expectations, they are more likely to become repeat clients and share their experience on social media and with their friends.

This sharing of experience is what we know as word-of-mouth advertising/marketing. Because of reviews and experiences being aired on social media and review sites, it is easy to get a tarnished online reputation. Keeping your brand promise leads to brand loyalty, repeat purchases, brand loyalists, increased brand awareness and new customers. Failing to keep your brand promise results in bad reviews, no repeat purchases, no brand loyalists (but some haters) and no new customers.

Failing to keep your brand promise leads to a failed business.

Brand promises that do and don't work. Many businesses are good at understanding how important it is to keep their brand promises. For example, Ford promises affordability while Bentley promises luxury. If Bentley launched a £15,000 car, it would go against the Bentley brand promise and consumers would not be happy about it.

This scenario happened to Mercedes a few years ago when a low-end (cheap) Mercedes hit the market. In 2011 their tagline was 'The best or nothing', but they can't be the best and low-end. Their brand promise didn't match up, and Mercedes brand loyalists were not pleased.

How to communicate the brand promise. If you get it right, you will grow your brand through consistent communications and actions. These will directly communicate your brand promise, evoking feelings that deepen your brand trust and loyalty.

My favourite example of this is the delightful little duck-egg blue box. This box fills every woman's heart with glee when she receives one as a gift. If you haven't guessed it, I am speaking of the Tiffany jewellery brand.

The Tiffany duck-egg blue packaging carries with it the Tiffany brand promise. Their iconic brand, which is loved by many, has been built over time, and has delivered time and time again. It brings reassurance to the giver and the receiver of the gift. You instantly know that the duck-egg blue packaging contains high-quality, fine jewellery from a brand that promises the best.

Brand personality

What do you want to be known for?

Think about specific personality traits you want prospects, clients, employees and joint venture partners to name when describing you or your organisation.

As you know, this section of the book is called 'Hollywood Branding'. It is all about attracting clients around you like paparazzi round a celebrity. And your personality has to be conveyed in all that you create to achieve Hollywood Branding. You need to craft your brand personality. What kind of personality do you want it to have (your and the business's brand)? You need to think about what you are and what you want to be.

Here are a few comparisons to get you started:

- Formal or funny?
- Big or small?
- Boring or surprising?
- Reserved or outspoken?
- Stylish or classic?
- Premium or inexpensive?
- Masculine or feminine?
- Rigid or flexible?
- Young or mature?
- Charming or chummy?

You have to craft your brand. You cannot leave it to others to craft it for you. Your brand personality is what will help you stand out from the crowd and attract a tribe and clients who love you. People will try your product or service because of the benefits and your niche specialism, but they will be loyal to you if your personality is attractive.

It is no different from the dating game. You often go on a first date because you feel attracted to your date, but you grow to know, like, trust and love them because of their personality traits. Your branding is what will get people to want to know you further. Your brand personality will be what gets people to fall in love with you.

The easiest way to do this is to know yourself. You have to be the Powerful You; share your brand personality and understand that the only way to get a loyal tribe is to be Marmite – some will love you and some will hate you.

Once you have determined and stand strong in your personality, it's time to have fun and start designing around it. Create a set of visuals that show off your personality and style. The key visual elements are colour, typography and imagery. Yes, this is the stage where we can talk about logos, websites and colours.

Just as words create voice, so do visuals. Certain colours can make you feel happy or sad; fonts can be seen as feminine or masculine; images can be dark and mysterious or inviting and happy. Other elements can be seen as emotionless, which works well if you have other strong traits. Think about the typeface Helvetica or the colour beige which take on properties of surrounding elements.

Here are a few common elements and the personalities that are attached to them:

Colour:
- Warm colour: happy, inviting, stimulating, active
- Cool colour: calm, relaxed, serene
- No colour: stark, bleak, simple
- Complementary colour: harmonious, soothing, trustworthy
- Contrasting colour: bold, active, impactful, chaotic, energetic
- Saturated: intense, bold.

Typography:
- Serif typefaces: formal, trusting, mature
- Sans serif typefaces: informal, agreeable, modern
- Script typefaces: typically feminine, elaborate, special
- Uppercase type: impactful, bold, pushy
- Lowercase type: informal, relaxed
- Title case type: trustworthy, solid, expected.

Images:
- Images with no borders: informal, fun, surprising
- Images with heavy borders: strong, impactful
- Images with fine borders: expensive, mature, honest.

Other elements:
- Square elements: formal, expensive, mature
- Rounded elements: informal, fun, casual, modern
- Alignment: common alignments are more formal (left and justified), while right and centred alignments are more casual and chaotic
- Space: more space creates a sense of organisation and harmony while tightly packed elements seem cluttered and chaotic.

Now that you are thinking about brand personality and what different elements can mean, how do you create your brand personality? Put it all together across a variety of platforms. Understand and know the characteristics and tone of your brand. What are the five key phrases that define the brand? How can you communicate in that way?

Make sure that when communicating on behalf of your brand you are consistent in voice and style. If your brand is silly and fun, this should apply to both the website and Twitter feed, for example.

The biggest mistake I see both start-up and established businesses make is that they scrimp on crafting their brand personality. And remember this personality is for life, so craft it well.

Brand story

Behind every start-up is a story, whether you choose to tell it or not. The reason you are reading this book is your story: the things that got you to this moment in time.

Before looking for investors, customers, profits, press coverage or even having a perfected product, every start-up has at least one unique and valuable asset: its story.

To understand why you are where you are in your life, ask yourself some questions. You might want to ask yourself:

- Who am I?
- Where did I come from?
- What was my journey to today?
- Why am I doing this?

Whether you are answering these questions for yourself or for your cofounders, your company's story has more power than you might imagine.

I know that when I stand on stage and tell my story, the impact it has on the audience is phenomenal. Immediately they start to resonate with me and feel aligned with my brand more. My story is the most powerful tool I have today to get people to sit up and listen to me.

Your potential clients want to know why you care so much. It might be that you have a personal connection to the problem you solve or it might be that you have a strong vision of a different and better world. If you are setting up a business to chase money then I suggest you go back to your day job. A business built around chasing money is not sustainable. It is difficult enough to start and scale a company; money alone will not keep you motivated.

The process for writing your story:

First tap into your emotions. If your story is devoid of emotion then people will not 'feel' it. You will not feel it. When you write it, do not think that you are writing it for others, but for yourself. Do not see it as a marketing piece.

I found the more feelings I put into writing my story, the more therapy I gained. In fact, writing my story healed many of the wounds that had been left from experiencing it.

Next list the turning points. We don't want to hear about what school you went to (unless it is relevant) or your earliest memories, but we do want to hear about the major turning points in your life. The places you went when you were standing at a crossroads and the decisions you made marked significant turning points in your life.

Then go deep into the first draft. Write everything that has happened to you that you think might be relevant. One memory will lead to others popping up, so trigger that action. You may not use all of the information, but there was purpose behind every moment you think is significant – even if it doesn't make the final edit. See, hear and feel it.

Make sure you use all your senses when you are remembering back through the decades. How did that feel? How did it look? How did it sound? Again, using the senses will not only enable you to get more detail, but you will enrich your writing.

Have a theme. Your story will have a theme, and as you write, it will become clear what yours is. Themes could include acceptance, courage, perseverance, cooperation, compassion, struggle, honesty, kindness, loyalty and rags to riches. If you have a theme which is the central part of your story it will be easier for people to understand it. You may discover more than one theme, but there will be one which stands out above the others.

And most importantly, it is about telling your story. If you are anything like me you may have hundreds of parts to your story. You may have wept for England and been an emotional wreck as you wrote it, but have you really told your story?

As you begin pulling all your work together, make sure that you are thinking about who is going to be reading it. Will your story connect and resonate with your readers? Does it demonstrate why you are the person to help others overcome pains they are going through? Nothing is so warm and inviting yet so poignant and challenging as a powerful story well told.

Your story needs to be written and shared. It is your responsibility to tell your story, not only for your sake, but for the benefit of others. Stories change people's lives. They shape entire cultures.

Brand visibility

As iconic as your branding (logo, website, colours, etc.) may be, there is nothing more iconic than having a name that stands head and shoulders above the noise that is in the marketplace. The most powerful tool I know for getting clients and being remembered is to have something I call a Stage Name.

The problem with your current name. Yes, you have a problem. Although you were born with a name, it is often forgotten. How many times do you feel like a number in your corporate job with no one knowing your name? When you go out and meet someone new in a meeting or networking event, the chances are they will forget your name in an instant.

Your name in your new business is your future. It will represent how seriously you will be taken, and if you chose a great brand name (Stage Name), it will become an extension of your brand, just like mine has with The Start-Up Strategist. It's pretty clear that it does what it says on the tin.

A Stage Name will sell for you and position you in the marketplace as the go-to person in your industry – the niche celebrity as I call it. By positioning yourself as the niche celebrity using a Stage Name you will condense the timeline of getting known and start to attract clients faster and more easily than if you use your birth/marriage name.

- When you create a stage name for yourself a few things will start to happen to you:
- You will be known by that name and easily remembered
- You will instil confidence in your clients because your name reinforces your service
- You will become more confident because you are proud of your name
- You will be positioned instantly in prospects' minds and have to sell less
- You will attract media attention easily as they'll have a 'hook' for a story
- You will be Googleable and not have to compete with others for a high Google listing
- You will be easy to refer even if people forget your name.

'Oh, you want to get fit but not go to the gym? You need that woman – you know, the one called The Body Engineer. Her name escapes me, but if you google it I am sure you will find her... '

And *voilà*, she is found.

Here are some examples of Stage Names. Some are of famous people, others are of my clients who have positioned themselves for niche celebrity status:

- The Social Media Queen
- The Juice Master
- The Book Midwife
- The Naked Chef
- The Visibility Queen
- The Start-Up Strategist
- The Body Engineer
- The Clarity Coach
- The Autism Specialist.

Another example of where Stage Names really helped position and develop an iconic brand was with the Spice Girls. I bet anyone over the age of fifteen can name all the Spice Girls, not by their real names, but by their Stage Names – Sporty, Baby, Posh, Scary and Ginger. How much easier are they to remember than their real names of Melanie Brown, Melanie Chisholm, Emma Bunton, Gerri Halliwell and Victoria Adams (later Beckham), especially when they first came onto the market and needed to position themselves quickly in the charts?

So as you work through the book and gain clarity on your niche and how you help people, see what Stage Name would fit with you – one which you could wear as a badge of honour. A Stage Name will position you more quickly than anything else and enable you to become a niche celebrity.

Step 3: Profit Packaging

As I started my start-up journey I didn't know what I was doing. I had no plan, no goals and no idea of how I was going to make money.

All I did when I started was get myself a cheap laptop computer, a dongle to get the Internet, and a three-page badly-designed website (created in return for me copywriting the designer's website). Then I started networking. I had no idea what I was doing or where I was going. And things did not change for two years. In fact, for two years I struggled to make more than £1,000 a month in my business.

Many would have given up, but I was determined to create a life for myself and my children that would give me freedom and untold happiness. So I looked to others for inspiration and started on my personal development journey.

The nuggets of gold that I am about to share with you in the following pages will change the way you set up your business and will determine your financial success. If you don't have profit in your business, you don't have a business. If you don't have a business, you don't have freedom.

I will explain how Profit Packaging is key for good cash flow, and how selling your services by the hour and not by the value you provide will send you broke – as it did me until I learnt otherwise.

As you read through these pages your vision for your ultimate freedom-based business will keep evolving. Increasingly you will gain insights into your own potential and how to package up knowledge and talents that will create repeat business, driving profit margins higher and higher as your business evolves.

Escalating your way to profits begins by helping your clients overcome their highest needs or three dominant problems. Think of it a bit like the school system that we have. In the UK we start off at nursery, spending a few hours a week outside the comfort zone of home. Then we go on to primary school, secondary school (or middle school), sixth form and university, and some go on further to specialise.

Each level of education that we undertake provides a higher degree of detail and expertise. If we were to be thrown into sixth form or university without partaking in the previous educational establishments, our minds would explode. We would understand nothing, and we would collapse under the pressure of the information overload.

The escalating (or graduating) system that schooling uses is a perfect example of how to run your business. Ideally every successful business has a defined product or service that includes a low price entry-level product and a succession of more expensive and sophisticated products/services with more sophisticated experiences.

Case Study

An example of this is Apple.

One of the many ways Apple has drawn millions of new customers into its business to become loyal fans is through the profit packaging method that it uses. The journey that you go on from the moment you become an Apple customer is seamless.

It starts with the iTunes download, a free product available for PC and Mac. This allows you to buy and download music with a few keystrokes. Apple literally puts its shopfront in its customers' hands.

Once you have downloaded iTunes you try the iPod/iPhone. From the iPhone you purchase an iPad, then a Mac Book and finally the hardcore Apple fans purchase the iMac, all the while getting more and more hooked into Apple products and syncing everything together for seamless usage. This means that the moment you start on the Apple journey you are getting to know, like and trust them and spend thousands of pounds on a suite of synced products that constantly needs updating.

As you can see in the case study, Apple takes you on a journey, and this is the Profit Packaging model I speak of.

I too have this model, which many of my clients and tribe have used as an example of how they can package up what they offer. I am going to talk you through the different parts required so that you too can benefit from the Profit Packaging magic.

Packaging your business

Each product that you create must pre-sell the next step. Step one will build the need for step two; step two will build the need for step three; and so on, just like the education system. This technique is called seeding and is practised by every successful business. It is one of the least pushy ways to sell as you guide customers through the process rather than pushing them. You also package up what you do based on value rather than the time you take to implement it or the materials used to create it.

Think about Apple as a product example. Apple Macs and PCs are fundamentally the same thing, yet Apple computers can be three times the cost and Apple's Tribe do not bat an eye. To Apple's Tribe the perceived value of an Apple computer outweighs that of a PC.

The levels of Profit Packaging. Two hundred years ago it was the age of agriculture and farming. Agriculture was streamlined and crop rotation was introduced. We know it as the Agricultural Revolution.

One hundred years ago we moved from farming to cities. In these cities we built factories – big factories – and steam power took over. The pace of the world quickened and more products became readily available for everyone. This was the Industrial Revolution.

Fast-forward to the late 20th Century and the Technology Revolution hit us. No longer do the wealthiest people farm land or produce mass quantities of products in factories with bustling production lines. The wealthiest people simply have big ideas that change the world for the better and use technology to help their ideas spread like wildfire. They package up their talents and passions and find a way to help overcome a need or a problem in the world. They have a purpose in life and do meaningful work.

So in this section you will find out the exact formula you need to package up your products and services so that you provide value and get profits.

Creating products from your ideas. There are many ways you can share your ideas. The least effective way is one person at a time, and the most effective way is reaching as many people as possible with one product or service.

If you package up your knowledge into an information product, you can create it once but sell it many times. And if packaged properly it can have a high-perceived value with very little cost.

Step 1 – Intro Products. In its most basic form, think of something like a CD, DVD, eBook or short email course. This is what we call an 'Intro Product'. Intro Products are free or very low priced products (less than £100) that start to form a bond with your ideal client. This step attracts your prospects to engage with your company and gives you an opportunity to demonstrate your knowledge and expertise in a way that makes them want to find out about what else you have to offer. A mixture of free and cheap options is essential not only to build your email list quickly (so that you can continue to market to prospects) but also to offer a low barrier of entry for people to engage with you further.

Step 2 – Foundation Products. The Foundation Products are set at a higher price point than the Intro Products. They could have a similar format to the Intro Products but with a higher level of information or detail. Ideas could include an email course or a membership site.

They can be priced between £100 and £500 and can be paid for outright or on a monthly membership, e.g. £37 a month for twelve months. If you aim for under £100 a month then your conversions will be higher as it is a low barrier to entry.

Step 3 – Master Products. Master Products are high-end sophisticated products and services, typically involving high touch points between you and your clients. – think sixth form and university if we look back at the schooling system. In Step 2 you will have given prospects a piece of your system or methodology; in Step 3 you give them the complete system with finer detail and a full solution to their problem/pain.

Master Products will contain your nuggets of gold and they deliver huge value. They could include one to one consulting, templates, workshops, webinars, workbooks, live events – use your imagination to create something jam packed full of value. They can be priced anywhere between £500 and £30,000 or more depending on your ideal customer and the value you provide. Do not limit how much you charge for your Master Products; create your products around your ideal customer's pain. One of my clients, a life coach, charges £35,000 a year for his one to one coaching and travels all around the world helping high performing people get more out of life.

Please note that, because your Master Products can vary in price, it may be you offer a couple of solutions, one that incorporates group consulting, and another that incorporates one to one consultation. The most successful way to leverage your time for maximum income is to help people in multiple numbers. A group of ten to fifty people each paying you £4,000 will make you more profits than a one to one client paying you £7,500. Both take the same amount of time investment, but the return on that time is phenomenally different.

In each step you are solving a very specific piece of your customer's problem. You are meeting them at each development stage and are taking them on an escalating journey to go from pain to solution at a pace that suits their budget and commitment.

By using this model, you will see your ability to leverage your time and money dramatically is exponentially increased. Skip Profit Packaging and you will be left burnt out and poor.

Skyrocket your success. Whether you are just at the beginning of your journey and have yet to make the leap to entrepreneur or have been running a business and struggling to make money, getting the profit packaging model outlined will give you the confidence to market your services/products with ease.

Don't worry about how you will create the products yet, or even what each product will include. For now all you need to do is brainstorm ideas for the products so you can complete the foundations of your business. These foundations will create a business; without them you will fail.

Signature system

What is a signature system?

Your signature system is the unique system/steps/process you take your clients through when you work with them.

Whether you realise it or not you probably have the same way of working with each client, and this is a roadmap of how you take your clients from pain to solution. Do not overcomplicate it. Your signature system will create a container for your body of work, and creating it will give you even more clarity.

A signature system will raise your profile and have you seen as the expert. It will give you a plan for taking your clients from A to B, give your clients confidence in your product or service as they will know what is involved and ensure you stand out from the competition. You will become more than a health or life coach; you will get known for your processes, and clients will find it easy to understand what you do. You can systemise each product so clients can easily choose their options. Life becomes easier; you no longer have to 'wing it'. You will make more money as you can create different package options, will be consistent and get great results, and great testimonials.

Uncovering your story. Signature systems can be created through your own story. Sometimes your 'rock bottom' is what brought you to where you are today. Maybe you are in your industry because you overcame a problem, and are now your best walking testimonial. Your journey to where you are today could be the reason you are so good at what you do. Maybe you saw a gap in the market and you knew you could fill it. Maybe you experienced something and it was so bad you knew you *had* to do it better.

Why do you do what you do, the way you do it?

How did I create my signature system? I learnt from others about my industry via books, YouTube, seminars and programmes, seeing what worked. Added to that were trial and error, practice, consistency and mistakes I made.

What was missing? Creating my own way, adapting others' ideas that didn't work, mixing and matching ideas, tapping into my unique genius and downloading new ideas.

When I analysed the exact steps I took with every client to get them from idea/struggle to profitable business, I realised there were predictable steps that needed to be taken every time.

In 2012 when I put my first signature system together it looked very different to what it does now. Let me share with you:

The twelve steps to clients in abundance (2012–2013):

1. Mindset
2. Mission and USP
3. Knowing who your clients are
4. Message
5. Your offering
6. Your website
7. Marketing
8. Creating assets for your business
9. Creating a blogging diary
10. Social media platforms
11. Creating a plan
12. Systems for growth.

FreedomPreneur Methodology: (2014 to date)

1. Diamond Clarity
2. Hollywood Branding
3. Profit Packaging
4. Authentic Marketing
5. Wealth Breakthrough.

Journal your story

As previously mentioned, your signature system is often in the journey that got you to where you are today. So let's journal your story.

Question 1: where were you before you started on your journey? (Sick, overweight, hated your job, lack of abundance, financial rock bottom? List all experiences you have ever had.)

Question 2: what were your trials and tribulations? (What worried you, kept you tossing and turning at 3am in the morning, made you feel sick? What were you obsessing over?)

Question 3: what happened to get you on the path? (How did you end up doing what you are doing?)

Question 4: what did you study or learn to support you in your transformation (books, courses, seminars, lessons, YouTube)?

Question 5: what did you have to release and let go of (certain foods, got divorced, left your job, met your soulmate, gave up habits, etc.)?

Question 6: where did you end up? (Where are you now?)

Question 7: what was your process? (What did you do first, second, third, etc.?)

Question 8: were there any themes, e.g. awakening stage, cleansing, releasing, transforming, systemising, analysing, reviewing, monitoring? Why did you reach the point you are at today?

Question 9: what are the wonderful life experiences, adventures, journeys and joys you have experienced? This is your chance to brag about how great they are. Example: you've met your soulmate, married, travelled the world, lived in cool places, had children, had home births, been on retreats, gained your best body, made money, quit your job, got a degree, followed your passion, worked with amazing clients, etc.

Question 10: what was the result of the process and transformation? (Where are you now? What has come from it? What were the *exact* steps you took?)

Step 1:
Step 2:
Step 3: etc.

Confidently answer the question 'Who am I?' and stand in it for all the world to see.

Knowing who you are and confidently standing in yourself will magnetise money, ideal clients and amazing opportunities your way. Stop being afraid of being seen and heard for who you are and allow the abundance into your life. Many FreedomPreneurs are afraid to be who they really are because they are afraid about what others will think, say or do.

Is your signature system in your story? Mine was as I lived my story, and it created a large proportion of my signature system. Even if yours isn't, you now have your 'About Me' page written. If it is in your story then the next section will help you get more clarity (and it's still your 'About Me' page).

Where to put your story:
- Signature talks
- Your bio on LinkedIn
- Your bio on guest blogs
- Your bio on press releases
- The 'About Me' page on your website
- Tele-classes/webinars.
- You will create an intimate and dynamic relationship.

Creating your signature system from scratch. Even though you may not have worked with clients yet, you have to start somewhere. It is time for you to plan something rather than guess. You know your stuff – it is your talents and your experience that have led you here today.

As you start to work with clients, you will be doing the same things each time even if you are not consciously aware of it. If you have yet to get clients then you can now create a signature system and propel your success far faster than if you don't have one. If you have more than one stand-alone product you may want to create a number of different signature systems for each product to be easily understood.

Questions to ask when creating your signature system. What kind of processes and tools could you share with prospects? What kind of information, knowledge, wisdom did/will you teach them? Do you give workbooks/handouts? Where do they ultimately end up? What are the results they will have? What were the exact steps you took them through for the desired outcome? If you were going to take someone through the process, what would the steps be? Examples: goal setting, visioning, meditation, body movement, inner healing work, basic foundational nutrition knowledge. (Fill in the blank of your expertise, art, movement, photography, tantra, money stuff, visualisation, essential oils, business analysis, planning, etc.)

How to create signature system magic. Get sticky notes, pens and a wipe board. Write down everything you would like to teach/implement. Brainstorm down as much as you can – you may have fifty sticky notes or more. Next, categorise into as many similar categories as needed, then pair down into five to seven categories. Place in an order – beginning, middle and end. Sit with your sticky notes for a few days; move them around.

Enjoy and have fun. Signature systems support your ideal clients in feeling held, safe and contained. A step-by-step process is easy for the western world to get their heads around.

Businesses are successful because they are built on solid structures, leveraged systems and repeatable plans. We can add in flow after we have created systems. And if no systems are present we have to recreate the wheel every time, which is exhausting and provides no certainty for us or our clients.

Building your signature system will mean that you have a strong business. You will have something that you can hang your hat on, and your clients will feel safe and secure when they buy from you.

Once you have created your signature system you can leverage it in the following ways:

- Free gift on your website written as an eBook
- Backbone to a webinar
- Signature talks/seminars
- Stand-alone course
- Teach others your system
- Franchise/hire 'mini yous'.

Finalising your signature system to paper:

- Put it into three, five or seven steps so you don't overwhelm prospects (not twelve as I had to start with – way too complicated)
- Make sure your system accomplishes something of huge value
- Create each step with a sentence or two as an explanation
- Create a diagram so it's easy to understand.

Knowing your signature system will solidify your business, ground you and support you in knowing and feeling your value.

Don't delay – begin working on your signature system at once. Imagine the ripple effect your body of work in the form of your signature system will make on the world.

Step 4: Authentic Marketing

Stop looking for information to consume and learn more from, start creating assets that bring you and your tribe joy – write, produce, speak and share.

In the following pages you will get an overview on some of the most effective ways to market your business. You will be able to download some templates to help you; take the strategies I share and implement them with ease.

Where necessary you may wish to outsource some of your marketing to a specialist or a marketing/admin assistant. I am assuming, though, that you may be watching the pennies at the beginning of your FreedomPreneur journey. With this in mind, the marketing ideas I will share with you in this chapter cost little or no money, just your time.

Before I speak to you about effective marketing platforms I would like to share with you some of Google's insights. These insights will enable you to stand head and shoulders above your competitors, create assets for your business and make more sales with ease. Most people are not aware of these insights, and for this reason their businesses struggle and they make life far more difficult than it needs to be. The information I will share here is essential to make the most out of your marketing activities.

Let's dive straight in as this information is gold.

Zero Moment Of Truth

In 2011 Google introduced to us the Zero Moment Of Truth (ZMOT) and described a revolutionary way in which consumers make decisions about brands and whom they are going to buy from.

Whether we are shopping for cornflakes, concert tickets or a business coach, the internet has changed how we decide to buy. Today we are all digital explorers, seeking out ratings, reviews, videos and in-depth product and service details. We are seeking proof that a certain supplier is the one that we should use.

The Google study found that most people do not buy on their first touch point with a product or service. In fact, the first time someone sees your website, brochure or social media advert isn't going to be the moment they make a decision to buy. Google found that a buyer needs an average of seven hours of interaction across eleven touch points and four locations.

This information is so important when you are planning your marketing activity. Gone are the days when you can place an advert in the yellow pages and have someone call you up and buy from you immediately. The options for a potential client to compare the marketplace are limitless. So you need to show that you are the go-to person in your chosen niche. You also need to ensure that potential clients can get to know and like you before they want to do business with you, which is why you need to have seven hours' worth of consumable content available and easily found.

The only way to have seven hours of consumable content is to create information material that enables your prospect to find out more about you and be assured you have the answers to their pains.

This consumable content, when created into information material, becomes an asset to your business.

Nic Rixon and Darren Shirlaw of Shirlaws use 'Income follows assets' as their catchphrase. They shared it with one of my mentors Daniel Priestley, who in turn shared it with me. This principle had a huge impact on my business success, so I delved further into it and found it originally traced back to Warren Buffett advising about the real estate market.

Income follows assets

Today I share the principle of income follows assets with you. So how does this principle work?

If I was to ask a typical FreedomPreneur how they create more income, they would probably say they need to make more sales and carry out more marketing activities. Most struggling FreedomPreneurs think that income follows sales and marketing. As a result of this wrong thinking, a lot of their time and energy goes into hunting and chasing new business, working long hours and exhausting themselves in the process. This often leads to small businesses being left in the struggle zone.

The reality is that income follows assets.

This short sentence revolutionised my business and helped me grow my small and struggling coaching company to a fast growth training and mentoring business in less than four years. Since 2012 I've helped launch hundreds of small businesses.

Let's use real estate as an example.

Imagine I own a one-bedroom house. This one-bedroom house

typically rents out for £1,000 a month. If I went to the best estate agent, created the best website and did the best marketing I could for the house, the most I could rent it out for is £1,100 per month – possibly £1,200 per month if I invested heavily in sales and marketing, a great copywriter, branding, and threw in the furniture too. But no matter how much money I spent to market it, the house's income would be capped at £1,200. And imagine I'd paid £10,000 for sales and marketing, the yield I would get on this would be insufficient for an extra £200 per month.

However, what if I spent that £10,000 on renovating the house and turning it into a two- to three-bedroom property with a nice kitchen and an en suite bathroom? The rent would automatically increase to £2,000–£3,000 per month. If I then took out basic classified adverts and did the marketing myself, I could triple the income the house generates and have created a bigger asset in the process.

Most businesses are caught in the struggle zone because they have only built a one-bedroom house which produces a capped amount of income. The solution is to turn your business into a bigger asset so you can have a bigger income without having to pay thousands for sales and marketing, spend hours networking and have coffee meetings hoping to grow your business, which of course was how I started growing my business , leaving me stuck in the struggle zone.

So what is a business asset? It is anything that passes the hit by a bus test. If you were hit by a bus, would your business survive and still be profitable?

I turned my service-based business into a product-driven business with product assets. This meant that the business relied less on my time and attracted many more opportunities. If I am ever hit by a bus (God forbid), my business would still be of huge value to my clients and it would still attract different investors to enable it to grow again.

This means that your business needs to be built not on sales and marketing, but on creating assets that make sales and marketing less expensive, easier and of better quality and value. The real question, therefore, is how do you create assets for your business, especially as many businesses are service-based and created around the founder? This is where we need to tap into the intellectual property that is inside the founder's head (and the team they build up around themselves). And we do this in a number of ways.

You are about to be taken on an asset journey. I want you to imagine you are your client. How might your client interact with you? I want you to remember the Zero Moment Of Truth. It is time to remember that your client needs to consume seven hours of content over eleven different touch points.

Website

A website is your online brochure. Often this is the first real point of contact with a prospect. Your website is an asset, and if it contains plenty of information, you can rack up content consumption time and build a relationship with a prospect.

With this in mind, time is of the essence when it comes to getting your website up and running. All too often I see new businesses engage a website designer and still be working on it six months later. If you imagine that your website is your shop window, if it is not there for people to look into, then they will move on to the next shop window and look in that. As we've learnt, buyers have a need to consume information when researching whom to buy from.

Today creating a website isn't something you should *probably* do, it's something you *must* do. Whether you decide to build a website yourself or outsource the design and build, you still need to understand the steps to the process.

Your website is an asset so don't skimp on the quality. We discussed branding in 'Hollywood Branding', and you need to ensure that your brand follows through your website. But this doesn't mean you need something complicated. The bells and whistles can wait, but you must get something up so that a potential client can spend some time researching you on your website.

What you need:

1. **A domain name.** Choosing a domain name is like naming a baby. It needs to be right, because you will have it for the lifetime of your business. It also needs to fit in with your business. So is the website name your name, the name of your product, or the name of your company? These are decisions that need to be made before you take your business to market, and thinking it through properly can save you a lot of heartache in the future.

You may find you need more than one website as your business grows and the more you become a niche celebrity. At the time of writing this book I have two websites: one is www.AmandaCWatts.com and the other is for my main programme, www.FreedomPreneurBusinessAcademy.com.

If you chose a domain name such as welovebagels.com but your business's name is Bagel Factory, it won't bring people to your site easily. Make things as effortless for your potential and existing clients as possible, beginning with your domain name. In this case it would be www.bagelfactory.com. When starting your business you also need to research Trademarks and Intellectual Property law. Whatever domain name you choose, please check you are not breaking a TradeMark or opening yourself up to litigation.

What if the domain name you want is already taken, yet not being used? Well you have two options if this is the case. You can try adding another word, such as 'the' or the city in which your business is located, to the domain name. Using Bagel Factory as an example, you could use www.thebagelfactory.com or www.bagelfactoryLondon.com. Alternatively you could try contacting the individual who already owns the domain name and ask them to sell it to you. This may prove costly and not be fruitful, but it's certainly worth a go, especially if they are not using it for themselves. You can find out who owns the domain name by going to www.whois.net.

2. Turn your website into an asset. No longer do I want you to think of your website as a way for people to find out how to contact you. I want you to think of it as your prime real estate. You need to make sure you are not creating a one bedroom house but a mansion.

So what can you put on your website to turn it into an asset?

Blogs and articles

You have to write blogs and host them on your website. Blogs are an asset; here are the main reasons why:

- A blog is a simple way to connect and share information with your potential clients. It is your direct communication channel

- Your blog will fuel search engine optimisation, which means that you will show up higher on Google in the rankings. Your aim is to get onto page one when someone Googles for help
- Your blog is the heart of all your marketing efforts. The content you use in your blog will be what you post on Facebook, Twitter, LinkedIn, etc.
- Your blog gives you a voice. It gives you a place to position yourself as the expert and comment on new products and services that you may be introducing
- Your blog will give you a personality. It will give you a chance to rally your tribe around you, and start to attract people who believe in what you believe
- A blog will create a two-way conversation. It encourages interaction, comments and feedback
- A blog can be fun. If you are passionate about your topic you will find that you will enjoy writing about it. If you are not a natural writer, you can have videos as your blog (more on videos later)
- Writing a regular blog will help you build confidence, relationships and sales. Potential clients will come to you as a reliable resource for information on your industry and then want to buy from you. If you have enough educational blogs then potential clients can easily rack up a few hours reading them. Remember it is all about spending seven hours with a prospect
- Blogging will sharpen your business focus. The only way to blog successfully is to know whom you are writing for and why. If you have completed the 'Diamond Clarity' module, then blogging will be, dare I say, easy
- Blogs are a very cost effective marketing investment. As you know, the best way to market your business is through creating assets. A blog is a long-term asset

■ Blogging is inspiring. You will start to see that your ideas and thoughts can generate hundreds of blogs a year. You will be inspired to write the more you write.

What should you have in a blog? A blog should take the reader on a journey. It should be easy to read and understand, and offer value.

There are two things that stop people from blogging regularly. The first is not knowing how a blog should read, and the other is not knowing what to write. Both of these problems I am going to address below.

There is a lot of white noise on the Internet. Remember that every blog you write needs to be an asset, so although you need to write often, you also need to write well. It is very easy to churn out a 300 word blog without making it easy to read and informative. If, however, you lay out your blog well and provide interesting content that can help people, your blogs will be shared, read and commented on.

To make sure you have credible blogs you need credible ideas. Below I list nine ideas for blogging for your business.

Insight blogging.

One original thought is worth a thousand mindless quotings.

Insight blogging is where you can share insights and original ideas and trends that are happening in your industry. For insight blogging you must know your industry inside out. When you set up your business I hope it is/was in your business sweet-spot, so I am assuming that you are talented and passionate about it. If this is the case then insight blogging will make you very credible.

Piggyback blogging. Piggyback blogging is where you jump on something that is in the news and write about it. If a topic is trending and there is an angle you can link to your business then piggyback blogging is very effective. It will get a lot of attention if you write and publish it quickly, but this attention will decrease over time as the subject matter becomes old news. This is not evergreen information.

Announcement blogging. If you have something to say that is breaking news then this would fit under the announcement blogging heading. Please try and steer from the announcement being about you or your company. (Nobody really cares if you have won an award. It's great for credibility, but expecting people to read a blog on it is pushing your luck.)

Announcement blogging works well when you know something about your industry that others do not yet know. The downside of announcement blogging is that it is hard. You need to be one step ahead of everyone in your industry, but try and do it as often as you can as it will make you very credible.

Link blogging. This is really easy as you do not have to think of anything to write yourself, you can just provide links to other exceptional information. For this reason please do not do it too often as you will be encouraging website visitors to leave your website. It is a time consuming practice, but it can be fun to compile.

Ideas could include: forty bloggers to watch in 2016; ten places to get your free photos from; ten books that will change your life.

Photo blogging. Using photos is a great way to tell a story and get your message across. Photos are easy to consume and are great for businesses that sell something visual, for example photographers (duh!), jewellery designers and artists. If you use photos to tell a story it can really help get your message across. Even if you are not selling a physical product that photographs well, you can have some fun creating storyboards to tell your story. This is so easy now with the technology we have at our fingertips.

Review blogging. Review blogging is a great way to position yourself as the go-to person in your industry. You can review books, whitepapers, newspaper articles – whatever you feel you can summarise and write about, you can use review blogging to do so. But, make sure you have a strong opinion so that you stand out from the crowd, otherwise your opinion will get lost. The stronger your opinion, the stronger your tribe will be.

Top ten blogging. This kind of blog will be shared lots, for example top ten ways to:

- Get more customers
- Get more followers on Twitter
- Get fit in the next thirty days
- Find time for your family
- Achieve happiness in your marriage.

The list is never ending. Top ten blogging is easy, fun and enables you to share quality information with your readers.

Guest blogging. If you don't ask, you don't get. Guest blogging is something you have to ask to do. Try and get an opportunity to write for other people's blogs as this will help drive traffic to your website and your social media platforms. You can use any of the examples above to construct your blog. Guest blogging is brilliant for Google and search engine optimisation. It is also brilliant for your credibility.

Video blogging. I will cover this in more detail after I have shared how to construct your blog.

How to construct your blog. Remember this is not just a writing exercise but a marketing campaign. Think about the amount of time your audience may have to read your articles and keep them short and informative. Avoid stretching out articles – people do not appreciate fluff! It is better to have more articles than long boring articles, but do write more than 300 words for each article as you want to be seen in favour by Google and other search engines.

Insider tip: if you cannot work out a length, look at other people's articles in your industry. If they are successful then follow their formula.

Article structure. What makes an article different from a page on your website, a sales pitch or a press release is the structure:

Title. A summation of the contents addressed throughout the article. A few things you need to consider when writing/choosing a good title:

Avoid misleading titles. Make sure the title represents the article well. It is imperative that the readers know what they are about to read.

Use the appropriate tone. The tone of the article should be reflected in the title.

Make sure your title stands out from the bunch to grab the attention of the reader. Thus, it is best to avoid using clichés and proverbs; instead, opt for informative titles.

The length of the title is ultimately dictated by the subject of the article, but keeping the number of characters fewer than seventy-five is good practice since most of the popular article directories do not accept longer titles.

Tweak the title once the content has been written.

Introduction. This is the first paragraph of the article and introduces the topic under discussion. It provides a little background information if required. Basically, it serves as a brief introduction to the article itself.

Once you have the topic for the article and you have done your research, you can proceed to writing the introduction. It is actually more effective to write the introduction before the title, but either way can work.

Easy steps to ensure you write the best possible introduction:

1. Main points. In bullet points, write down what are the main points you want to discuss throughout the article.
2. Connect the different points you have written down. Depending on the subject this could form a short narrative story or a fact sheet. Once you have an idea of what connects your entire article, you basically have the introduction in your hand.
3. Editing. Most people tend to write the whole article in the introduction when what they need is the essence of the content. Keep this in mind when editing and cut the introduction down till it cannot be cut anymore.

Once you get the hang of these steps you do not have to follow them every time. They are just meant to get you in the proverbial 'groove' of things.

Body. This is the content of the article – what is popularly considered the meat of the article.

Once you have done your research and introduction paragraph, the rest of the article (body) becomes easy. You need to lay out the information you are discussing to optimise its readability.

Tips on how to achieve this:

1. Bullet points: Bullet points break up the information and are easier to read for time-starved Internet users. Wherever you can, break up the article's most salient points into bullets for an easier read.

2. Subheadings. If you cannot afford to break the article up into bullet points, you can always create sections with subheadings. Consider the subheadings created in this section as an example and break up the article into sizable chunks that are reader friendly.

3. Paragraphs. Even if you are writing an article with personal stories and experiences you should break the story up into paragraphs. Huge chunks of text together look heavy to the reader, but by simply putting your article into paragraphs you can avoid them.

Some salient points you need to remember:

References. If you are quoting from another article, reference the original content. When you are including any statistics in your article it is also important you name the source. Support any claims/propositions you make in your articles with citations and statistics.

Plagiarism. Plagiarism is a definite no. Reputable article directories will not accept plagiarised articles. Even in cases where plagiarised articles are accepted, search engines will reject the duplicated content.

Spelling and grammar. Use the spell check feature available on all word processing software, but don't depend on it. Check spellings with a dictionary and ensure they are consistent throughout. It reflects badly on you if you have spelling or grammatical errors in your articles. To make sure your grammar is accurate, hire a proof reader or editor, especially if you do not feel confident in the beginning.

Other than that, the article should be written with flair and confidence. Use adjectives and personal anecdotes where needed. This will help the reader connect with you on a personal level.

Closing paragraph. The last paragraph of an article holds a definitive conclusion to the article and is imperative. A proper conclusion will help readers get the full picture. A good closing paragraph should have the following factors addressed:

1. Summarise the findings of the article. If it is a review article, the closing paragraph should include the findings of the review and why it was carried out. Likewise, if you have a how-to article or a list article, you need to summarise your findings in the conclusive paragraph.

2. The closing paragraph should reinforce the core statement of the article and include a call to action (buy your book, read another of your blogs, check something on your website...).

3. Satisfy the reader. You need a good conclusion that summarises your main points, so as not to leave the reader abruptly. Make sure you have answered their possible concerns and encouraged or directed them to more of your content they may be interested in.

The worst mistake you can make is abruptly ending the article. It can cost you traffic. If you choose to outsource the article writing, ensure you use writers who provide a good closing.

What else to avoid when closing your article:
- Do not present any new ideas
- Do not state any new facts or information

- Do not use bullet points or subheadings
- Do not make the closing paragraph too lengthy. Keep it short, sweet and to the point.

Author's bio. This includes links, author's credentials and any other information about the business. The author's bio is part of what is referred to as the resource box with article directories. It is exactly what it sounds like – a brief introduction to the author – and aims to fill one of the flaws of online marketing, which is the absence of face-to-face selling/service. People like to know what they are buying, but the savvy consumer today also likes to know whom they are buying from. The author's bio bridges that need.

Here are a few things to keep in mind when writing your author's bio:
1. Write in the third person. This helps build authority subtly.
2. Avoid unnecessary embellishments or adjectives; keep it professional.
3. State only the relevant credentials. There is no need to tell people you played professional football for a year if you are trying to sell them sunflower oil.

Most article directories have a separate box at the end that you can fill out once with your author's bio and an appropriate picture if possible. Once you have saved this information, you can publish any number of articles and the information will appear at the end of every one. You can edit or update your information whenever you want through your account and/or profile settings.

And that is how you start blogging. In fact, if you choose to embrace blogging you can do so without even having a business. Find something you are passionate about then blog about it. Many great businesses started as a blog and transformed into a business as they gained followers.

Video creation

Show, don't tell. This is the simplest yet most powerful lesson a storyteller can learn.

There was a time when video was only an afterthought for most of us. It used to be that you needed to go into a studio and pay a small fortune to have a three minute video shot with a polished end result.

Then things changed, so much so that now you can record and edit videos on your smart phone and upload them to Facebook and YouTube at the click of a button. YouTube is now the second largest search engine after Google.

If you have a solid budget for creating your video then great, but if you don't, and if you want to have video uploaded regularly, then don't think slick, think value. Consumers are more focused now on the content rather than a video that looks pretty.

I am assuming by now that you are seeing how the 7/11/4 principle can work well when building a relationship with prospects and how easy it can be to create content of value. If there is one thing I would recommend more than anything else, it is embracing video to share your expertise and make you a niche celebrity.

So what length video should you have for maximum impact? Honestly, there is no right or wrong here. Some people want to consume your material for hours on end while others want a quick one to two minute fix, but bear in mind studies have shown that viewers tend to lose interest at the two minute mark as their attention span dwindles.

Attention spans are short online. Regardless of the length of your video, users will typically only watch the first ten seconds before deciding whether to continue watching or move on. So you've got to make those first ten seconds count. Don't wait until the end to push the viewers' hot buttons; push them early, and often.

Testimonials on video. As you get good customer feedback on your product, service or book, why not capture this enthusiasm on video? With smaller cameras, phones and digital delivery, creating video testimonials is easier than ever.

By having testimonials on your website, YouTube and Vimeo, you will be able to show your prospects the client transformations that you have facilitated. A video testimonial is the strongest testimonial there is.

Trailer. Think movie trailer. This is great for promoting books, but it can also work for products and services too. A video trailer is a short professionally-produced video that highlights the main points and provides just enough of a hook to provoke a desire for the whole story.

Relationship videos. These are content-rich in nature. Examples of relationship videos include video newsletters and video blogs where you, as the expert, deliver your content in video format. Internet users are becoming increasingly accustomed to reading e-newsletters and blogs – you can take this one step further by constructing videos.

How-to videos. How-to videos are tutorials for your product or service. Showing customers how to solve a problem is much more effective than getting them to read the solution in print. Creating these types of online videos often cuts down on service calls and refund rates – you can determine the content based on your customers' needs. Using a how-to video to cover various help topics or FAQs is a beneficial idea.

Webinars. Some of you may not have come across webinars before. For those of you who are new to them, they are a presentation, lecture or workshop transmitted over the web. You will probably hold them live to start with, and as you deliver them you will record them and post many of them to YouTube for people to stumble across and see your expertise.

For those who are shy of the camera, webinars or teleseminars can be a great option as you can avoid showing your face and be guided by PowerPoint slides. This is how I started my YouTube channel, how I got confidence sharing my knowledge on the Internet and how I attracted a lot of my tribe to my email list.

To get started on webinars here are some platforms you can try:
1. GoToWebinar
2. WebinarJam
3. Zoom

Budget should no longer be a reason to stop any business owner creating video assets. Fear may kick in, but as I said right at the beginning of the book, use gumption to give you courage and then dive in. Confidence will come.

LinkedIn SlideShare

Seventy million professionals trust SlideShare to learn about any topic from subject matter experts.

Founded in 2006 with the goal of making knowledge sharing easy, SlideShare joined the LinkedIn family in 2012 and has since grown into a top destination for professional content. With over eighteen million uploads in forty content categories, it is today one of the top 100 most visited websites in the world.

Share your insights and get noticed. Show what you know through a presentation, infographic, document or video. Visual formats help you stand out and resonate more with your readers. When you upload to SlideShare, you reach an audience that's interested in your content – over 80% of SlideShare's seventy million visitors come through targeted searches. This can help you build your reputation with the right audience and cultivate more professional opportunities.

SlideShare is a wonderful place to share your assets and it is used by serious professionals. Unlike Facebook or Twitter, those on SlideShare are there to learn and get information.

Case study taken from the SlideShare website

'With the right methods and approach, just about anyone can reach one million views on SlideShare.'
JONATHON COLMAN, FACEBOOK CONTENT STRATEGIST

Colman, a long time SlideShare user, published thirty-seven presentations over seven years, ultimately reaching one million views. His most popular presentation, part of a SlideShare upload campaign entitled 'What I Carry: 10 Tools for Success', has fetched more than 330,000 views.

He shares his advice for reaching one million views on SlideShare:

Invest time in the SlideShare community. Follow other users, like and comment on SlideShares you admire, and subscribe to your favourite topics.

'SlideShare isn't just a repository for PowerPoint files. It's a community. And like any community – real or virtual – you get out of it what you put into it,' he says.

Learn from others. With eighteen million uploads and forty million registered users on SlideShare, there are a lot of examples and people to learn from. See how others engage an audience, and do the same.

Support others by sharing their work. If you share someone else's deck on social media platforms, they're likely to share yours. And the more your content is shared, the closer you are to reaching one million views.

E-books

Writing an e-book is quick, cheap, and it's easy to produce. An e-book is a book in an electronic format that can be downloaded to a computer, Mac, PC, laptop, tablet, smartphone, etc. It can have numbered pages, pictures and be exactly like a printed book. There is no restriction on size.

Writing an e-book is a powerful asset and a smart move. Let's take a quick look at why this is so.

E-books are delivered almost instantaneously. Prospects can purchase, download and start reading them within minutes, without even leaving their chair. For this reason, having an e-book is a powerful tool to get your knowledge into your prospects' hands.

An eBook can be consumed easily and is portable. Your prospects can carry a whole library of e-books and spend hours consuming your content. E-books can show links to videos and blogs you may have written if you want to impart more information. They are easy to sell and distribute, and are great incentives for prospects to provide an email address in return for a free download.

Our success is solely dependent on how many assets we can create in our business that our potential clients can consume to enhance their relationship with us. A 7,000 word e-book should be easy for you to write if it is based on your passions and talents. It can then be turned into a PDF document for download on your website for free and you can upload it to Amazon for selling.

Don't overthink the tools you will need to create the e-book or you may be stopped dead in your tracks. Just start writing and sharing your knowledge in this portable book format and people will see you as an expert. You will not get away with writing an e-book that is just a couple of hundred words, though. Remember the book you provide is all about positioning and value.

Most people will download your e-book if the title speaks to them and they feel value will be inside. If you get the title wrong then you will not get people to download it, and your list will not grow. So here are some examples to help you get it right and grow your list using your e-book asset:

Use emotional 'pain points', emotional motivators and clear benefits to fill in the blanks and brainstorm out compelling headlines.

How To [Mundane Task] *That* [Rewarding Benefit], for example: *How To Get A Mortgage That Saves You Money.*

How I [Accomplished My Goal], for example *How I Improved My Memory In One Evening.*

If [Specific Pain Point Situation Is Happening] *Then* [Worst Fear Might Be True], for example *If You Experience Lower Back Pain While Sitting Then You May Need Surgery.*

What To Do If [Pain Point Is Happening], for example *What To Do If You Notice Your Husband Looking At Other Women.*

Ten Mistakes Most [Customer Description] *Make* [In Situation] *And How To Avoid Them*, for example: *Three Mistakes Most Men Make In The Kitchen And How To Avoid Them.*

How To Get [Result/Benefit In A Certain Time Without Risk], for example *How To Get Out Of Debt In Ninety Days Or Less With This Simple Guaranteed System.*

How To Get [Eliminate Specific Pain] *Without* [More Pain], for example *How To Lose Thirty-three Pounds Of Fat Without Torture Diets Or Hard Exercise.*

Why [Common-Sense Approach] *Doesn't Work And What To Do About It*, for example *Why Diets Don't Work And What To Do About It.*

How To [Turn Problem Magically Into Benefit], for example *How To Lose Weight By Eating More Food.*

Sales brochure

Are you a real business?

By having a blog on your website and getting people to join your list, you will start to grow your business and attract interest in what you are doing. However, one of the biggest lessons I learnt when starting my business was that I was only going to get a sale when I had a conversation with someone over Skype/phone or met them face-to-face. And further still, they only converted to clients easily when I had a brochure printed. A brochure was a key asset to getting a sale. It made me a real business in my prospects' eyes.

A brochure is perfect to share when having a meeting to explain your product or service. It beats the online format that can be ignored or difficult to read, and it beats a PowerPoint presentation as you can leave it with the prospect. It turns your product/service into a tangible 'thing'. And when you have something that people can easily buy, signing up to your programme or your course can become an easy transaction.

Again, I don't want you to dwell on the tools to create the brochure. This should be outsourced to a designer and will cost very little. I remember I had 150 copies of my first brochure printed and it cost me less than £100. (I also designed it in Word in two hours, but I wouldn't recommend that.) Find a good designer who can bring your brand to life and you will get more clients.

Here is an overview on what to have in your brochure:

Title page. A title page says what the product/service is. It includes a clear target market and a list of benefits.

Clarity and credibility. What you do and for whom. The FreedomPreneur Programme brochure clearly advertises a training company that helps corporate employees set up a business and start making money. It also talks about my extensive background in providing the tools and strategies to achieve this, how it is an award-winning product and how I am an award winning coach many times over. I include credible case studies and testimonials as proof of what the brochure says.

Problem. The FreedomPreneur Programme brochure delves into the situation of the corporate world and how people feel when starting a business. It talks about the three dominant problems clients have before they come to me.

Solution. This is where I introduce the five step methodology. I demonstrate how it is delivered and introduce the details of the programme.

Call to action. The call to action is based solely on a primary objective, and it's not always about getting people to sign up. As the brochures have developed over the years and FreedomPreneurs Business Academy has grown, my objective has become to get people to join me on an exploration session. You might want someone to visit your website, download your eBook or sign up. Whatever you choose, it must be about the next step you want them to take.

Sign up form. There have been times when I have not taken a sign up form with me to a meeting and regretted it. A sign up form is essential. Even if you do not plan to bill the client immediately, having a sign up form will turn them from a prospect into a client.

Make sure you ask for their name, address and payment details.

Again don't fuss over tools for taking payment (options can include PayPal, Stripe and GoCardless to name a few), just get the prospect's details and then worry about how you will bill them.

Terms and conditions. You will need terms and conditions for those who sign up to your product/service. You may need to include legal disclaimers, so I suggest seeking the advice of a professional.

Having a brochure will turn your business idea into a tangible product for people to buy. It will make you a real business.

Conclusion about business assets

As you can see, assets are going to be your marketing collateral to enable people to consume your information for seven hours, eleven times and over four different mediums. The assets I have outlined in this book are not exhaustive. There are many different ways you can create tangible business assets for people to enjoy, this book being yet another great example. It is one of the touch points in our journey together.

If you can create blogs, videos, audios, eBooks, books and brochures, your business will thrive. People will be able to consume your information and make an educated decision about working with you, even before the sales call. This makes sales easy, and fun.

Sharing your assets with the world. In this section we have spoken about creating valuable assets for your business: blogging, webinars, videos, eBooks and brochures. I recommended that you don't obsess over the tools to distribute these assets; the work for distributing them can be outsourced. If, however, at the beginning of your journey you wish to learn how to use these asset distribution tools, then here is a list to get you started.

Business Tools

Social Media Marketing

Facebook	facebook.com
Twitter	twitter.com
LinkedIn	linkedin.com
SlideShare	slideshare.net
Instagram	instagram.net
Periscope	periscope.tv
Snapchat	snapchat.com
Buffer	buffer.com
Hootsuite	hootsuite.com
Sprout Social	sprout.com
Meet Edgar	meetedgar.com

Video

YouTube	YouTube.com
Wistia	Wistia.com
Vimeo	Vimeo.com
Camtasia	Camtasia.com
VideoScribe	Videoscribe.com

Landing Pages (webinars, downloads, etc.)

LeadPages	Leadpages.net
Unbounce	Unbounce.com
ClickFunnels	Clickfunnels.com
OptimizePress	Optimizepress.com
GetResponse	Getresponse.com

Customer Relationship Management

Infusionsoft	Infusionsoft.com
Ontraport	Ontraport.com
Campaign Builder Pro	Campaignbuilderpro.com
Active Campaign	Activecampaign.com

MailChimp   Mailchimp.com
AWeber   Aweber.com
Constant Contact   Constantcontact.com
HubSpot   Hubspot.com

Productivity
Evernote   Evernote.com
Asana   Asana.com
Slack   Slack.com
Dropbox   Dropbox.com
Google Drive   Google.com

Graphics for blogs
Canva   Canva.com
Word Swag   Wordswag.com
Unsplash   Unsplash.com
Pixabay   Pixabay.com

Outsourcing
Fiverr   Fiverr.com
Upwork (Elance-oDesk) Upwork.com
Virtual Angel Hub   virtualangelhub.com

Webinar Platforms
Webinar Jam   Webinarjam.com
GoToWebinar   Gotomeeting.com/webinar
Zoom   Zoom.us
Google Hangouts   Hangouts.google.com

Raise your profile

As well as creating business assets, there are other ways to attract clients to you. The stronger your profile, online and offline, the more opportunities will come your way.

As a new business, the easiest way to raise your profile is to be seen, online and offline. You need to embrace social media marketing to ensure that when you are Googled you come up, and people can consume your material at their leisure.

But there are other ways to make some noise too. In this following section I will cover options for getting PR coverage, public speaking and a fool proof strategy for face-to-face networking.

Press release

No matter what industry you are in, getting press coverage is one of the most powerful tools for driving prospective customers to purchase from your business. It can provide you with the credibility to sell a book, secure paid speaking engagements and attract customers worth tens of thousands of pounds. It is your single best tool for generating the credibility you need.

A press release is designed to capture journalists', producers' and editors' attention so much that they request to do an interview with you, get you to write a feature column or contribute to a TV or radio segment as a guest expert.

However, for you to get featured successfully in this competitive market, crafting a press release is only one very small piece of the puzzle. To stand out you need to consider various critical elements prior to hitting send on your campaign.

Getting media coverage for your business is a valuable asset. It gives you the ability to charge more for your products and services. It lets you create credibility that instantly increases your conversion rates. It lets you leverage your time and money, and most importantly, it puts you in front of hundreds of thousands of potential customers in one hit for next to nothing.

The great news is most businesses have a newsworthy angle that will get them coverage. They just don't know what it is, nor do they have a true understanding of why the media continues to feature their competitors over them or why their current media efforts fail to bring in new revenue.

Let's begin by taking a look at the seven critical mistakes most people make when pitching for media.

1. Your story isn't newsworthy. To secure coverage you must have a newsworthy story. Launching your new product/service is hardly captivating – especially if thousands of others are doing the exact same thing every single day (which I hope they are not as you have created a niche).

PR tip: list the media you would love to get featured in, then identify the ten top stories that particular media has focused on in recent times. Dissect the key elements you believe made those stories newsworthy. Now revisit your proposed idea – does it carry weight or does it require work?

2. Marketing message unclear. Whether you're an author, speaker, consultant or entrepreneur, you must have a marketing message that captures the hearts, minds and wallets of your prospective customers.

By ensuring that you and your business stand for something, you will draw the media to you immediately. If your cash flow is poor and the media keeps ignoring you, one of the core reasons for this is likely to be that your marketing message isn't compelling enough for them to wish to engage you or feature your product/service.

3. Credible competitors. When promoting yourself as an expert, credibility reigns supreme. Zero credibility means that you won't get taken seriously. This means that you need to work on the quality of your work, word of mouth and getting featured in places in which key influences will notice you, and fast.

If journalists aren't returning your calls or responding to your press releases, it's because they do not portray you as your industry's leading figure. This is typically due to key credibility factors being left out of bios that accompany your releases – elements many seem to fail to focus on that can get you over the line effortlessly.

PR tip: create the assets that we mentioned earlier, have video readily available and share your blogs with journalists. The more you position yourself as an expert, the sooner you will become a niche celebrity.

4. Your content is uninspiring. Media must do their research when interviewing for a story or conducting a feature. If they don't, it is their heads on the chopping block and could lead to a very public demise. They conduct their due-diligence by visiting your website and social media pages. If they are not moved by your current content, or worse still cannot find any current content, e.g. articles, status updates, etc., they won't move forward with an interview.

Writing articles for your blog isn't only about writing for prospective clients, it is about writing for those who have influence over your larger markets, including the media.

5: Weak personal brand. Your personal brand is one of the key deciding factors when it comes to the media selecting you to be interviewed. If they see that your blog and social media presence lack strong opinions or professionalism and personality, they will not contact you.

Creating a Hollywood Brand is the first step to getting media attention, and writing a press release is the second. It doesn't matter what you write, if you do not appear credible, it will not fly.

6. Another 'me too' brand. It takes less than ten seconds to conduct a Google search to see that you have thousands of competitors. The challenge therein is how do you say the same thing, but say it differently?

There are few unique products/services in the marketplace, but a great twist on an old concept can bring new life to it which will be followed by new cash flow. When offering your opinion to the media, do not say the same thing your competitor would say. Find a new angle, say it with more passion and provide a highly educated and intriguing point of view.

7: Fail to convert coverage. Generating media attention without an offline and online sales conversion process is business suicide. One cannot be implemented without the other. They complement and support one another in generating cash flow for your new business. Conversion is a critical element that needs to be embedded throughout your entire business model to enable you to benefit from regular income and ongoing sales.

Any media interview conducted (where possible) must drive prospects into your sales funnel so you can grow your database and meet your sales objectives. So think about your call to action, and the journey you want people to go on when they read about you.

How to get media successfully – your essential checklist. Before you begin writing your press release, tick off the strategies below you currently have implemented to ensure your likelihood of success is high.

Media strategy clearly outlined. You know your objectives and you're clear on how to reach them.

Pitches are prepared. You've researched a list of potential pitches you can fire off to secure coverage.

Social media strategy. Your social media strategy supports the messages that you'll be sending to the media.

Press release distribution. You've got more than five ways to approach the media to capture their interest.

Content marketing strategy. You have in place a 'native advertising' strategy that will support your efforts and boost your sales significantly.

Prepared email communications. You have some pre-written email communications you can fire off to prospective outlets that could feature your story. The communications need to strike the right chord, not too pushy or laid back.

Interview preparation. You know exactly what to do and how to prepare for an interview with the media to ensure you secure new sales and elevate your status as an expert within your field, otherwise known as the niche celebrity. Putting in the groundwork doesn't have to take hours and hours of preparation when you have the right tools in your hands, as my clients who have consistently been featured in the media know.

To help you get started, here is a simplified press release template. This format will assist in your probability of appearing in the media.

For Immediate Release

For additional information contact: (insert your contact details here, the person/company sending the press release)

Press Release Heading

Write a powerful headline that is in alignment with the target media (your Perfect Fit) you wish to send this to. Write twenty headline ideas before cutting them back to your top five, then three, then one.

Opening Paragraph

Write your most powerful opening in forty words or fewer. Create intrigue and interest via storytelling, e.g. local author airs controversial opinions on hiring a life coach. This introductory paragraph should also answer the questions of who, what, where, when and why. Get straight to the point.

Body of Contents

The paragraphs of your press release should be no more than three to four sentences in most cases. One or two solid quotes are a must in your release, perhaps from you, a business partner, a client or the person featured in your case study.

Remember, the release shouldn't be about your business but the stories connected to it, e.g. client transformations, 'hitting rock bottom' stories, expert opinions on a popular topic of the moment.

Your release should be written in a journalistic nature that emulates the style of the media outlet you plan to target. Before you write your press release, read the media you wish to submit it to and write it with them in mind as inspiration for your style.

Those serious about getting onto a particular TV or radio segment, or into a newspaper, magazine or blog, write out word for word their top story of the day/month. This will help you in fully understanding what they need and expect from contributing experts, segments and stories.

About you (the expert) and/or the business

Write a brief biography about you or the business. Keep it clean and pack it full of credibility factors that elevate your status as an expert.

This mark tells the journalist that they've reached the end of the press release and there are no additional pages to come.

Speaking

Public speaking is a powerful way to get new customers and leads, so be sure to incorporate it as a prioritised strategy.

As a FreedomPreneur who wants to be recognised as the expert, you will always be in a more powerful position at the front of the room on stage than in the audience. As soon as you position yourself on that stage, all eyes and ears will be on you, waiting for your insights, and you can reinforce your personal brand as well as your business brand. People tend to perceive speakers as being more 'important' than non-speakers.

So what do you speak about? Create a core talk (which I recommend is based on your signature system) that reinforces your speciality, and practise it. Then, come up with a compelling title for your speech. Remember, your presentation isn't a sales pitch; it's a way to showcase your expertise, so provide great practical information that is helpful to your listeners. Make the speech in lengths of twenty minutes, thirty minutes, forty-five minutes and ninety minutes. This will be a talk you can use over and over again.

Show confidence by using humour and letting your passion shine through. During your speech, your audience has the opportunity to meet you without obligation and get a feel for your personality, style, and expertise. The people who like your approach will either hire you, or spread the word about you and your business.

Please don't be scared. Nothing used to scare me more than standing up in front of a large group of people who were waiting to hear me speak about marketing. Now that I understand speaking is just helping and serving those who need me most, I find it so much easier to do.

Here are five ways to get speaking gigs:

Networking groups. There are loads of networking groups around, and many are looking for speakers. Get in touch and do the rounds to see who might be suitable for you. Don't worry if the gigs are not full of ideal clients to start with; practice makes perfect, so get as many gigs as you can. Google local networking gigs for results in your area.

BNI – Business Networking International. Love BNI or loathe it, a highly structured environment that really makes you work hard at networking, it works. You are accountable to generate referrals and accountable when following up on referrals people have given you.

You have to be a member if you want to speak at a BNI event.

4Networking, founded by my straight-talking friend Brad Burton. Brad is a best-selling author and the UK's number one motivational speaker. When he set up 4Networking he had a vision for a relaxed, fun and friendly networking environment to enable new and seasoned business owners to get clients and grow their networks. It took him seven years to have the overnight success you see today.

I made my own corporate escape over ten years ago, probably more abruptly than is strictly recommended, £25,000 in personal debt, zero savings, and on a point of principle I told my boss to 'shove the job up his arse'.

It was a wonderfully liberating experience... for those three hours whilst I drove home.

Who knew, walking out of a job, five days before Christmas, £25,000 in personal debt, no savings wasn't a smart move?

Apparently my wife did. Within three months of self-employment,

I was delivering pizza at weekend to keep my business afloat. The reason I'm saying this isn't to be dramatic, but to explain that if you are serious about your business success, you are, at the outset, going to have to do shit you don't actually enjoy.

In those formative years, my wife would whinge when business was slow that I should 'Go get a proper job, at least you know where you stand'. Tell that to the 25,000 steel workers of TATA, or the 15% of a global bank that have just been let go.

There is no such thing as job security anymore, it's a myth. Being employed is a bit like being self-employed, the difference is you've got one client, your boss, and if they decide they no longer want your services, through no fault of your own, you are gone.

Trust me, you're kidding yourself with the 'job security' thing; you don't know where you stand.

However, you know exactly where you stand when you are self-employed: fucking skint. Get used to it.

But you ain't going to starve to death. So what's the risk? As in the real risk? You can no longer afford the posh wine you are sinking each evening to mask the pain of the career you are not feeling.

The risk is, it doesn't work out and you can go back and get a proper job...which is exactly the place where you started from.

Anyhow, ten years on, absolutely no regrets, best decision of my life. Even the wifey acknowledges this... now, as I run a multimillion pound international operation, 3 business books under my belt and a 3rd career as a professional motivation business speaker. All this as a result of telling my boss to shove it.

See here's the thing when you are employed, it goes like this. Payday. Skint. Payday. Skint.

When you are self-employed it goes like this. Skint. Skint. Skint. Skint. Skint. Skint. Skint. Payday. Payday. Payday. It took me about seven years to get to the payday bit.

The business by the way is a company called 4Networking. A business networking membership organization.

When you do start your business off, you'll need more appointments, you need to get out of the box room as you go stir crazy aggressively waiting for the phone to ring. You start doubting yourself. Back in the old corporate days if you were bored you could go and speak to Janine on reception and still get paid. Working alone is soul destroying. So I created 4N to allow self-employed business owners to come together to swap contacts, leads, have more appointments and have a voice.

Back in 2006 we had one meeting, now my organization runs over 5,000+ each year all over the UK and thousands of members... I'm so glad I didn't 'Get a proper job'.

There really is no better way to develop your business than face-to-face networking. We are social animals, and we need to belong as a new business. Sitting in your box room aggressively waiting for the phone to ring is a quick route to despair – I should know, I've been there.

So get out there, go networking and unleash the passion you feel for your new direction, your escape. It's your best chance of success.

Brad Burton

Meet-ups. Find your people. There are thousands of meet-ups all over the world, and there will be one close to you. Both business and social meet-ups are perfect places to meet potential clients. Raise your profile and ask to speak at as many as you can.

Trade associations. Once you have practised your talks, then it's time to get in front of your audience in big numbers. Join trade associations that are relevant to your industry and have a room full of potential Perfect Fits to pitch to. Only do this once you are confident and have your talk smooth as silk.

Alternatively, you can run your own local event by posting flyers and letting your mailing list know or listing it on eventbrite.com for easy payment collection (yes, you can charge) and ticket distribution.

Remember your own event can also be virtual so don't feel you have to restrict who can come. You can be a global small business with ease, and live webinars can be a key factor in this happening.

So how do you get speaking opportunities? Make friends through networking. Networking is about building relationships, so your number one priority is to get out there and build deep lasting ones with people around the world. Get them to know and like you and then they will refer you.

Become friends with those who host or run networking events and offer your services to speak, and don't give in at the first no. Keep going until you get a yes. One speaking gig leads to another.

What to do after speaking at an event. Get names. Don't leave the room without growing your list. One of the biggest wastes of your time is speaking and not following up. Get people's emails and offer them a free gift (eBook, latest industry report, etc.) which you will send to them upon your return to the office. Then you add them to your list, continuing to market and provide high value content to them through auto-responders and other free gifts.

Speaking is actually the quickest and easiest way to grow your profile and your list.

Speaking tip: develop a speaker's sheet that you can send to groups. Create a page on your website that describes your expertise, background and speaking style. Include testimonials if you have them. Hand out information to your audiences about you, your company, and your services. If you have information products, you can often offer these for people to purchase at the event.

Public speaking is a powerful way to get new customers and leads. You'll find opportunities abound when you commit to getting yourself out there.

Networking

Ninety-nine times out of 100 people waste time at networking events that yield few or no clients. The strategy I outline below will enable you to have success and build your credibility and profile in less time.

First of all I want you to research five networking events that have your Perfect Fit attending. If you are unable to find a networking event with your ideal clients (my ideal clients are corporate employees so they don't tend to network at small business events), find one with attendees who have access to your ideal clients.

Then follow this strategy:

Pre event. Choose five networking events. Go to Twitter and follow each one, connect with the networking leader on Twitter and start to tweet before the event to make yourself known. If your chosen networking events have a list of people who will be attending (BNI and 4 Networking do), try and connect with them on Twitter too and say you will be going to the event. That way when you go to the event you will already have a relationship built with attendees and it will be less scary, less cold and you will have something to talk about.

Facebook. If you can connect with the leader and those who will be attending on Facebook then do so. Do not be worried if they do not add you on Facebook; they may keep it for personal friends only.

LinkedIn. As with Twitter, go and add the relevant people on LinkedIn and send them a message that you will be attending their networking event. See if they can recommend any good groups for reaching your ideal audience, and see who their ideal client is so you can refer people to them.

The more work you do before the networking event, the more you will get out of the event.

At the event. Relax, be friendly, and ask questions. Do not sell. The aim of networking events is to build relationships, not sell to people when you don't know them. Unless they ask about you, make the conversation about them. Knowledge is power, and with this knowledge you will know if you can help them, either with your services or by referring someone else.

Business cards. You will of course take business cards with you. But the aim when you are networking is to get information from others, not give your cards out willy-nilly.

When you get a business card from someone, take time to look at it, and then ask them if they would be happy for you to send them your free eBook/ informative newsletter/whitepaper/blog/etc. Then write on the card either yes or no (while they are still standing in front of you) so that when you get back to the office you can add them and send them whatever was fitting for them.

If you haven't already connected on the social media channels, make sure you ask people if they are on social media and if they would like to connect. This way you can continue the relationship after the event.

After the event. Send all who wanted to hear from you a 'great to meet you' email with the free eBook, etc. Add them to your newsletter list if they agreed to it. Connect on LinkedIn and Facebook, then jump on Twitter, follow them, do a shout out and share one of their tweets.

When you have added people on LinkedIn, make sure you tag them (when you look at your contacts, there is a tagging option). Use the networking event as a tag name so that they know where you met them first.

If there was anyone you really felt you connected with, arrange a one to one with them and spend thirty minutes getting to know them better outside of the networking event. If there was anyone at the networking event you really wish you could have spoken with but didn't, make sure you reach out to them and connect. LinkedIn is the perfect way to do so.

If you follow this simple networking process you will find you spend more time building relationships than if you just went to networking events, eating breakfast or lunch and wasting your time.

Do not lose sight of the power of deep relationships when building your business. Remember the four hours you spend at a networking event is very precious. If you imagine your time is worth at least £250 an hour, it cost you £1,000 to go to that event.

So to conclude this chapter on Authentic Marketing, let's talk about outsourcing. As your business starts to take off and your time becomes even more limited, you will need to outsource. Marketing can be kept in house, but if a lot of the 'grunt' work is taken from you, you can be left to do what you do best.

Create your business assets in draft form (brochures, website, etc.) and then get someone else to use their expertise to finish them for you. You will write the majority of your social media updates and put them in an excel spreadsheet with relevant links, but a VA can post them for you. You can create the strategies for growing your business, but you don't have to be the one pressing the tweet button. You may organise your diary and answer your emails, but one day you will realise that outsourcing this to a VA or PA will change your life.

This happened to me, and I would be lost without a PA. I no longer use a VA.

And remember, your marketing will be fruitless if you do not have a strategy and are not focused on making 7 hours of consumable content available to your prospects.

Step 5: Wealth Breakthrough

And so to the final chapter of the book and the last part of your FreedomPreneur plan. So far we have found you a business idea, worked on your ideal client, created a brand that means you stand out from the crowd and built profitable products for you to sell.

Our previous chapter was written to get you thinking in a completely different way about marketing. The only way you will have success is if you are authentically being visible in the marketplace, providing huge value and positioning your expertise – in other words, creating assets that people can consume.

This 'Wealth Breakthrough' chapter has been written so you can maximise your time in your new business, overcome procrastination, and have a plan for growth. Wealth breakthrough happens when you have a plan to ensure your business grows.

Freedom accelerator

Most people go back to their day job because they can't make any money in their new venture. This is down to the fact that they haven't completed every section in the FreedomPreneur Methodology and are not consistent in client generating activities. I have created the Freedom Accelerator for this reason.

Whether you are a start-up business or a seasoned entrepreneur, using the Freedom Accelerator will dramatically increase your sales and profits, and dramatically decrease the amount of wasted time in your business. It provides a daily/weekly sales and marketing plan that will consistently generate clients and prospects, enable you to complete projects and actions to create assets for your business and build foundations and strategies to catapult your success. Using a simple model based on goal setting, projects, evaluation and accountability, this twenty-one day programme will be one of the most important tools you use when trying to get more clients and create a profitable freedom-based business.

Why twenty-one days? Forming a habit takes time. You have to be consistent with doing the same thing over and over for it to become a habit: something you do naturally and easily. To be in your flow it has to come from within, not be forced.

The word about town is that it takes twenty-one days for this to happen. Whether this is true or not doesn't matter. Twenty-one days is the perfect amount of time for you to market your business consistently to make more sales and profits with a strategic plan.

So that is why I chose twenty-one days. This is not a one-hit wonder, though. Once you realise the power of the Freedom Accelerator programme you will want to continue it, time and time again. The results will propel you and you are likely to be consistently motivated to continue with the programme. At the end of the twenty-one days, make sure you use the following week to evaluate, plan and start another twenty-one days with new projects and actions. Imagine how many projects you will have completed in a year, and how consistent your marketing will be.

How it works

Overview. The ability to get clients quickly will transform your business. Starting a business can be scary, and creating a business with deep foundations, strategies and plans can seem overwhelming. No matter how many courses you take to learn how to get clients, if you don't take action and implement consistently all you have been taught, you will not grow your business. There is so much to do, and it begs the question: how much time should you spend doing it?

Where do I start? This is the most common question I am asked at speaking and networking events or during calls with potential clients. Should you be doing every piece of marketing activity there is to do, or should you pick and choose a few ideas and have a go at implementing them?

The answer is simple: the Freedom Accelerator definitely works if implemented properly. It takes you on a step-by-step journey to ensure that you market your business consistently, complete projects in a timely manner and are strategic in your thinking.

You will choose from a number of business projects and strategic actions, adding in the power of analysis and accountability every day, and will see yourself attracting clients and building your business.

The power of positive thinking

*'Whatever the mind can conceive and
believe, the mind can achieve...'*
NAPOLEON HILL

Each thought we have creates an energy flow around our physical beings. So if you're thinking 'I suck', then your energy kinda, well, sucks – and you attract sucky experiences.

The opposite experience occurs when you think high-level thoughts like 'I rock'. When you think and feel 'I rock', you exude an energy of confidence and attract great experiences into your life. Each thought you have informs your energy, and your energy manifests into your experiences. Your thoughts and energy create your reality – if you put those thoughts into practice!

And it is the same with attracting clients and growing your business. Your intentions create your reality, and if you have low-level thoughts about not having clients, you will not have clients. No matter how hard you market your business, you will not change your reality. You will ooze negativity.

But the opposite is again true. Be positive, create a strategic plan, and in doing so you will see yourself having opportunities, happiness and clients arriving at your door in droves.

So be positive when you are planning your business projects and actions. Know that by completing the twenty-one day programme you will attract clients, opportunities, joint ventures and raise your profile, which of course will mean you will have a successful freedom-based business.

Celebrating your wins. We 'like' posts on Facebook and 'favourite' tweets on Twitter, but being thankful every day for the small things in our lives is something that so many people fail to do. We are all on a healing journey of some sort, whether it is from illness, emotional blows or loss of loved ones. We all *want* our lives to be more fulfilled, richer, more connected with the world around us, yet we often fail to see the good in what surrounds us.

We can go through weeks and weeks of hard work without acknowledging what we achieved in each day, each week, and how far we have come in our business, and our lives. (This is even more prevalent when we work for other people.) But by changing the pattern of just existing and functioning and acknowledging the small wins, we add them up to big wins.

Wins can come in the form of having successful sales meetings, completing projects or creating products. You know what you need to achieve, and what will be a win for you.

You will not ever be an overnight success. Success comes from lots of tiny wins that propel you forward.

What about when you fail? You are going to fail. Let's get this clear in your mind. *You are going to fail.*

However, the more times you fail, the more you learn. It is imperative that you don't overthink your actions and live in fear of pushing yourself out of your comfort zone, as outside of your comfort zone is where the magic happens. It's where you become your most creative and achieve amazing things. Imagine how powerful you will feel when you experience new things and take action.

The first time you speak at an event you will quite likely be terrified. You may completely muck up and feel like you have failed. But remember every fail will result in a learning. What can you learn from your first speaking event, and what can you do better next time?

This is why every day you need to complete the two final sections of the Freedom Accelerator:

Section one: what did you achieve today (win)?

Section two: what did you learn today (possibly from a fail)?

The Freedom Accelerator Worksheet

My advice to you is to create a year long plan of what you need to achieve to grow your business and profits. Once you have created your plan, split it down into three month chunks. From these three-month chunks you can create projects that need to be completed. Some of these projects may take a day, some a week, some longer.

The object of having business projects is to ensure that you have all of your marketing material in place so that you can take clients through the marketing/sales funnel quickly and easily. Providing potential clients with plenty of information will help them go from prospect to client smoothly, so your business projects have to be chosen wisely. You need to choose three to concentrate on over the twenty-one day period.

If your business is a start-up, I would suggest that your business projects are initially chosen from each section outlined in the FreedomPreneur Methodology. A project could be one of the worksheets you have downloaded previously from this book, or it could be creating an asset from the 'Authentic Marketing' chapter, e.g. an eBook. Try to work through the five steps in the order they were presented. The reason for this is to ensure that you have built deep foundations into your business by not skipping anything I have taught you thus far.

Where to start. To decide what you need to work on, first think about where your business currently is. Do you have a clear target market? Do you have a description of services so that your clients can buy easily from you? Are you clear on what makes you different from your competitors?

If you can't answer these questions then you need Diamond Clarity. This will be the first thing you concentrate on.

Maybe you have your passion and purpose clear and have Diamond Clarity, but you have no clear branding guidelines and it's not clear what you stand for. If you are missing anything from the 'Hollywood Branding' section, make sure you go through and complete it first.

If you have a business already but haven't packaged up your services then work on 'Profit Packaging'. Do you charge for your services by the hour? If so the chances are you will become burnt out and exhausted and have a ceiling on your earnings. 'Profit Packaging' looks at creating packages for your services and having a clear idea about how to deliver your offering.

You need to start at the beginning. Do not skip any section, or you will not have a successful business.

Now choose three business projects (examples are below to get you started; a full list of examples can be downloaded from the website www.amandacwatts.com/book-resources), set yourself completion dates for them (within the twenty-one days), and make sure you have everything in place to take your clients through the marketing/sales funnel with ease.

Business projects:
1. Complete a Perfect Fit profile
2. Create a brochure
3. Write a downloadable eBook for website

Strategic marketing actions. This is the most important part of designing your Freedom Accelerator programme because without consistent strategic actions, you will not be able to move forward with the growth of your business.

You are going to choose eight specific and measurable strategic actions that you will be doing on a daily/weekly basis.

An interesting thing happens when you concentrate on marketing in a consistent way: you get results in unexpected places. When my mentoring clients work with me, they see clients and opportunities manifest within a week or two. The Universe works in mysterious ways, and as clients start to come out of the woodwork, it's as though it has recognised that you are working hard and has decided to reward you with amazing opportunities.

The power of strategic planning and action. Opportunities do not come out of the blue; they are a direct result of you having a goal, and a plan to achieve that goal. If you market your business and services consistently, taking action day after day, you will get business. Imagine if you call ten people a day, or go to the same networking event weekly and get yourself known, or write a blog every day and share it on social media. It won't be long before people are speaking about you, wanting to work with you or referring people who need you.

This phenomenon is so common that we have given it the name of Strategic Power. The existence of Strategic Power can help you enormously when choosing actions for your programme. Don't spend too long worrying about what to choose, just choose something and begin marketing your business with consistency.

Quick reminder: create, not consume. One of the biggest things I have ever learnt is to create not consume when building and growing a successful business.

Try to stop inhaling information about the world and business. Take twenty-one days off from watching the news, watching

YouTube or taking more courses; instead, concentrate on creating things that will enable you to do two things: serve current clients and get more clients.

Choosing your strategic actions. You will get better results if you don't spread yourself too thinly. Have a look at action examples below and download the full example at www.amandacwatts.com/book-resources.

Strategic Actions:
1. Write goals out daily
2. Post an update on Facebook Page daily
3. Write for an hour a day

Try to choose actions that complement each other. For example, if you are going to choose 'write for an hour a day' and write a daily blog, then it would make sense to choose 'update your website daily' and 'post on social media channels' as well. Then you can commit to a weekly newsletter as you will have created the content for it.

Include all of these actions in your strategic actions list.

Your strategic actions and business projects. If you have chosen to write an eBook as a project then writing for one hour a day is an essential strategic action. If you have chosen to find referral partners, then you need to ensure you are networking or contacting three referral partners a week/day, for example.

Your projects and actions should have the same outcome. Some of the actions you chose will be daily, some weekly and some several times each week. Daily means five times a week with weekends off, although if you choose to complete some or all of the actions every day, you will stand head and shoulders above your competition.

Remember the more work you put in, the more success you'll get out and the more freedom you should gain.

How to choose. Where are you in the FreedomPreneur Method and what do you need to focus on? Here are the main questions you need to answer to make the best possible choices:

Which marketing strategies will I be using and where are my clients? One thing I teach my clients is to fish where the fish are. Remember there is no point in going to networking meetings if your clients are corporate employees who never leave the office. LinkedIn might be a much better bet for you.

What is my desired goal? If you want to get speaking gigs then working on your speaking topic and bio project is a must. The strategic actions would be to speak to one networking/business group a week and spend one hour each week promoting your speaking events.

What am I actually going to do? You have to stretch yourself in order to grow yourself as a person and your business, but there is no point in choosing a strategic action or business project that you will not follow through on. For example, if you get stage fright then make sure you get some speaker training. Your strategic actions have to be things you are consistently going to do over the next twenty-one days.

What really pulls me? Some of the actions are going to be right up your alley. Choose these to start with, and measure the results – if you are coming from a place of confidence and really getting into your flow, then you'll get bigger achievements faster.

If you love social media and your clients are on it, then put together your strategic actions predominantly using social media. However, if you are not technically minded, outsource the social media to a virtual assistant and get out and mingle in the real world.

Whatever you choose, action it.

How much time do I have? I say to my clients that they should be working on their business for four hours a day if possible, whether this is writing, networking, creating products and packages or marketing online. If you are still working full-time while trying to plan and launch your start-up, choose activities that mean you don't have to take time off work.

How quickly do I need more clients? The more you push yourself and the bigger actions and projects you undertake, the more quickly you will get clients. The more quickly you need clients, the more aggressive you should be when implementing the Freedom Accelerator.

Remember to enjoy the journey using the Freedom Accelerator though, because if you are coming from a place of desperation, the Universe and potential clients will feel it. Set your goals, plan, then execute the plan strategically.

And finally make sure every day that you complete the two powerful and life changing sections: what did you achieve today (win)? What did you learn today (possibly from a fail)?

Deep breath in, and action! Once you have chosen your business projects and strategic actions, put them into the Worksheet PDF which you can download from the website www.amandacwatts.com/book-resources.

Freedom Accelerator Tracking Sheet

FREEDOM ACCELERATOR	DAY																				
START DATE:	1	2	3	4	5	6	7	8	9	10	11	12	13	14	15	16	17	18	19	20	21
BUSINESS PROJECTS (% COMPLETED)																					
PROJECT 1																					
PROJECT 2																					
PROJECT 3																					
STRATEGIC ACTIONS (Y/N)																					
1																					
2																					
3																					
4																					
5																					
6																					
7																					
8																					
TOTAL NUMBER COMPLETED																					

This is your essential tool for twenty-one days to build your business, form new habits and create new clients and a profitable business. Using the Worksheet will provide you with focus, evidence, direction and motivation to do the business building and marketing you need.

You could also arrange to do the Freedom Accelerator with an accountability buddy, or if you would like help putting the plan together, book a mentoring session to help you design your twenty-one day Freedom Accelerator programme.

Please email support@amandacwatts.com for further information.

Creating your Freedom Accelerator worksheet: projects. For each of your three projects, mark on a daily basis whether you have worked on them at all or how much you have completed them. Put a tick in the box if you have worked on them, and note the percentage completed beside it. You are aiming for 100% completed by the end of the twenty-one days for all three of your projects.

Some projects may take longer than twenty-one days to complete, so be realistic when planning and maybe split projects up into sections.

Strategic actions. For each of your strategic actions you need to put a Y or N depending on whether or not you have completed the action. Give yourself a free Y if you have a weekly action that needs completing, but only if you are definitely completing it that week. For example, if you have a networking event on a Thursday and your action is 'go to one networking event a week', then every day would have a Y because you will have achieved this action.

If you planned to attend an event and didn't go, then you need an N on every day. Whenever you reach the end of the week and you haven't taken a weekly action then you *have* to give yourself an N for it.

What are you aiming for? You are aiming for five Ys each week for each action. At the end of the day look specifically at and write down what you achieved today (win) and what you learnt today (possibly from a fail).

How to work the plan

Throughout the twenty-one days. Before you start choose your business projects and strategic actions and put them into the worksheet. For the next twenty-one days you will be working steadily on your business goals. Plan in rest days (maximum two a week), and plan in the time when you will be working on projects and actions. You may choose to spend your rest days working on your projects or spend time recharging your batteries.

Remember that this is a twenty-one day programme which means that you will have a week at the end of the month to relax properly, plan or start the programme again. You will be responsible for completing the daily actions on the days you have chosen to work, not the rest days you schedule in.

Set aside time in your diary to ensure you work on the programme every day.

Day 1: it's time to let the worksheet get you some clients and build your business. Plan your day at the start, factoring in time to complete your eight actions, and make sure you have your plan in front of you all day if possible.

Look over projects that need completing and daily/weekly actions you have to achieve. Which of these projects and actions do you have to complete today?

As you complete each action make sure you put Y or N into the box.

At the end of the day add up how many Ys you have got. If you have six or more Ys then give yourself a pat on the back and keep the actions as they are. If you have fewer than six, have a look and see if there is a reason for this. Make sure you complete your projects and add in the percentage of completion. These projects may take twenty-one days to complete, so any movement on them is a great start.

Ask yourself: were you short of time? Did you stretch yourself too much? If you were short of time, was this because you were unusually busy with clients, or was this the norm? If you were unusually busy on one day then crack on with your projects and actions and put it down to an off day, but if being this busy becomes normal, you may wish to scale back your strategic actions. They may be things worth putting on the backburner. Keep in mind, though, the less you do, the less results you will see.

What did you achieve today (win)? What did you learn today (possibly from a fail)? Eliminate the unusually busy from your life and redesign your strategic actions if you need to so they fit in with a typical day. Did you get any new clients or new leads to work on today? If so please write this in the win section.

Days 2–5. At the beginning of the day check the projects that you are working on today, then check the actions that you must complete. Throughout the day complete and tick off the actions, putting Y or N in the relevant box.

At the end of the day add up the number of Ys you have. If there are more than six, congratulate yourself. If not, see if there is a reason. Keep going, and if you fall off the wagon, get straight back on it the next day.

Remember it takes twenty-one days to make a habit so I suggest not skipping any days and always trying your best. You are doing this to create your life of freedom, so be truthful with yourself and watch your business grow and generate profits.

Days 6 and 7. These are your rest days, if you chose. Review your week and see where you are with your projects. Have you completed them? What percentage is completed?

Days 8–12. These repeat days 1–5. Complete the actions and make sure you are hitting six Ys or more. If you are getting eight out of eight then you are either not stretching yourself enough or you are a star.

I am sure it is the latter!

Days 13 and 14. These are your rest days, if you chose. Review your week and see where you are with your projects. Have you completed them? What percentage is completed?

Days 15–19. You are on the home stretch now. If you have been consistent with your marketing you should be seeing a difference – remember the Strategic Power effect. You may not see clients coming directly from the actions you have taken, but more opportunities will be coming your way, I'd bet my bottom dollar on it.

Make sure you complete the actions and keep aiming for eight out of eight Ys.

Days 20 and 21. These can be rest days, but if you want to be really successful why not give it one last push? Make sure you have completed your projects, make sure you have completed your daily actions on these days too and continue to complete your wins and learnings.

You did it, congratulations! Now is the time to review your business and marketing for the past twenty-one days. What were your goals and projects? How many new clients do you have, and how many of your projects have you completed?

If you completed the full twenty-one day programme without slacking and making excuses, then again congratulations. Completing the programme in itself is a measure of success, and if you found it really stretched you then you may have learnt more than those who easily reached 100% success.

Evaluation. Ask yourself what you have learnt about growing and marketing your business. What is the biggest thing you are grateful for?

What's the plan now? You have just completed a habit forming twenty-one day programme to help you launch and grow your business successfully. After you have celebrated and caught your breath, I suggest that you don't give up now. You have been doing this long enough to have formed a habit. Continue with the programme, print off new worksheets, start some new projects and choose new strategic actions.

If you managed to complete the Freedom Accelerator programme by yourself, imagine what you could do with a buddy. When you start again, this time get someone to do it with you. If you are consistently working on your business you will reach more people and make a much bigger difference to the world. And in the process, you will have turned your passion into a profitable business with an abundance of clients and be enjoying life.

I would call that a win.

Here is to your business success!

Go to www.amandacwatts.com/book-resources to download the Freedom Accelerator worksheets that accompany this chapter.

Summary

Congratulations on finishing this book. You now have a bullet-proof method to enable you to become a FreedomPreneur.

Each of us has a unique story and message that we can share with the world. We are all passionate about something, and we can all turn our passions into a freedom-based business.

You have always had the opportunity to become a FreedomPreneur. Until now you didn't have the methodology. What I have shared with you in this book is your ticket to escape your day job and live a life doing what you love. It is now your time to go out and make a difference in the world. Just promise me you will do it on your own terms and not jump from being a job slave to become a slave to your business instead. Being a FreedomPreneur is about having fun. It's about attracting opportunities to you. It's about crafting your own life.

Running your own business is a rewarding and exciting journey. Just like there is no end to the rainbow, there is no end to your FreedomPreneur journey. The good news is I am on this journey with you.

Join the Freedom Tribe here
www.facebook.com/groups/thefreedomtribe

Your Path To Freedom

Throughout the book you have been given resources to support your escape from the rat race and your journey to becoming a FreedomPreneur.

You will find all the worksheets at www.amandacwatts.com/book-resources.

To recap, the worksheets/audios accompanying this book are:
- Passion Challenge Programme (audios and worksheets)
- Finding your business sweet spot worksheet
- Perfect Fit worksheet
- Freedom Accelerator worksheets

FreedomPreneur Business Academy

The FreedomPreneur Business Academy is the home of online learning programmes as well as our flagship six-month business training programme, the FreedomPreneur Programme.

Find out more, visit: www.FreedomPreneurBusinessAcademy.com

The Author

Amanda C. Watts is a successful FreedomPreneur, speaker and author. She is the founder of The Freedom Tribe, and the FreedomPreneur Business Academy where she teaches new and aspiring business owners how to find their passions and start a business doing what they love. Her FreedomPreneur Methodology has helped 1,000s of people across the globe live life on their own terms and make a meaningful difference to the world.

Amanda was born in Brighton and grew up in Croydon, South London. She now lives in Surrey with her husband, two children, and her cat. From an early age she showed a passion for life, and with determination and her now unwavering belief, created a life that is fulfilled.

Amanda has designed her life and business to give her family and herself freedom in every sense of the word. She is a multi-award winning business coach and trainer, and has been an innovator in this field since she started her entrepreneurial journey in 2009. She holds formal qualifications in coaching and has worked with new and aspiring business owners from over forty industries, specialising in helping people escape their day job and make following their passions their full time job.

Since the creation of the FreedomPreneur Methodology, she has developed and honed systems and strategies that catapult a business's success. Her work has led to her becoming a mentor for Richard Branson's Virgin Start-Up programme, speaking regularly on escaping a day job and having a start-up that stays up, and being featured in national and international press.

She stands for living a passionate and freedom-based life.

If you want to know more about Amanda and her work, go to www.amandacwatts.com or follow her on her social media channels:

Twitter: www.twitter.com/amandacwatts
Facebook: www.facebook.com/TheAmandaCWatts
LinkedIn: www.linkedin.com/in/AmandaCWatts

Printed by Amazon Italia Logistica S.r.l.
Torrazza Piemonte (TO), Italy

10921309R00120